Grammar Dimensions
Workbook One

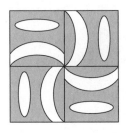

Cheryl Benz
Miami-Dade Community College

Mary Lou Kennard
El Paso Community College

Heinle & Heinle Publishers
A Division of Wadsworth, Inc.
Boston, Massachusetts 02116 U.S.A.

Photo Credits:

Photos on page 1 courtesy of Pat Martin
Photos on page 33 courtesy of Pat Martin
Photos on page 51 courtesy of H. Armstrong Roberts

Table of Contents

UNIT

1

The Verb *Be*
Affirmative Statements;
Subject Pronouns

Exercise 1 *(Focus 1)*

My name is Juan.
I'm from Mexico.
I am 19.
I'm single.
I'm a student.

I'm Julia.
I'm German.
I'm 19.
I'm single.
I'm a student.

My name is Rosa.
I'm Puerto Rican.
I'm 35 years old.
I'm divorced.
I am a teacher.

I'm Yumiko
I'm from Japan.
I'm 35.
I'm married.
I'm an engineer.

Put the sentence in the correct order.

E X A M P L E :   are/Juan and Rosa/Hispanic. *Juan and Rosa are Hispanic.*

1.   divorced/is/Rosa _____

2.   Yumiko/Japanese/is _____

3.   are/single/Juan and Julia _____

4.   35/the engineer/is _____

5.   is/the German/a student _____

6.   from Puerto Rico/the teacher/is _____

7.   Juan and Julia/19 years old/are _____

8.   a student/is/the Mexican _____

9.   Asian/Yumiko/is _____

10.   are/single/the students _____

1

Exercise 2 (Focus 1)

Fill in the blanks with *is* or *are*.

EXAMPLE: The students *are* 19 years old.

1. Yumiko _____ Japanese.
2. Rosa _____ 35 years old.
3. The engineer _____ Japanese.
4. Yumiko and Rosa _____ 35.
5. The teacher _____ Hispanic.

Exercise 3 (Focus 2)

Replace the noun phrase with a **subject pronoun**.

EXAMPLE: Julia is German. *She* is a student.

1. Julia is from Europe. _____ is German.
2. Juan and Julia are 19 years old. _____ are single.
3. Rosa is from Puerto Rico. _____ is a teacher.
4. The student is 19 years old. _____ is Mexican.
5. Japan is a country. _____ is in Asia.
6. My name is Yumiko. _____ am Japanese.
7. You and I are from Asia. _____ are Asians.
8. Mexico is a country. _____ is in North America.
9. Juan is from Mexico. _____ is single.
10. Rosa is a teacher. _____ is divorced.

Exercise 4 *(Focus 3)*

Rewrite the sentence using **contractions** (subject pronoun + *be*)

EXAMPLE: Juan is Hispanic. *He's Hispanic.*

1. Julia and Juan are single. _____

_____

2. Julia is a student. _____

_____

3. Rosa is from Puerto Rico. _____

_____

4. Yumiko is an engineer from Japan. _____

_____

5. Mexico and the United States are in North America. _____

_____

6. My name is Julia. I am European. _____

_____

7. Julia and I are students. _____

_____

8. Julia and Rosa are single. _____

_____

9. Yumiko is 35 years old. _____

_____

10. Juan is a student from Mexico. _____

_____

Exercise 5 *(Focus 4)*

PAIR, GROUP

1. Ask your partner the following questions:

What's your name?
Where are you from?
How are you?

2. Introduce your partner to the other people in your class.

Exercise 1 *(Focus 1)*

Fill in the blanks below. Then choose the correct answer to the puzzle.

Guess the Place

(1) _____ this place in Europe?

Yes, it (2) _____.

Is (3) _____ in Switzerland?

No, it (4) _____.

(5) _____ it in France?

(6) _____, it is.

(7) _____ it a museum?

Yes, (8) _____ is.

Is it (9) _____ Paris?

Yes, it (10) _____.

Is it (11) _____?

(the Hermitage, the Louvre)

Guess Who I Am

Am I female?

No, (12) _____ aren't.

Am (13) _____ an actor?

(14) _____, you aren't.

(15) _____ I a singer?

No, you (16) _____.

Am (17) _____ an athlete?

(18) _____ you are.

Am I (19) _____
soccer player?

Yes, you (20) _____

(21) _____ I from Brazil?

Yes, you are.

Am, I (22) _____ ?

(Pelé, Shaq)

Guess the Famous Couple

Are (23) _____ from the U.S.?

No, (24) _____ not.

(25) _____ we from Great Britain?

Yes, (26) _____ are.

Are (27) _____ part of the royal family?

(28) _____, you are.

Are we (29) _____?

(Charles and Diana, Romeo and Juliet)

Exercise 2 *(Focus 1)*

Choose a famous person. Imagine that you are that person. Your partner must guess who you are by asking yes/no questions.

E X A M P L E : A: *Are you an actress?*

                 B: *Yes, I am.*

                 A: *Are you an American?*

                 B: *No, I'm not.*

Exercise 3 *(Focus 2)*

Write five sentences describing yourself. Use the list of **adjectives** to help you.

busy	excellent	sick	healthy	ugly	young
angry	energetic	funny	overweight	strong	tall
happy	beautiful	poor	serious	weak	sad
thin	messy	rich	intelligent	loud	noisy
athletic	frightened	shy	outgoing	quiet	tired
organized	interesting	short	talkative	neat	calm
nervous	homesick	handsome	friendly	lonely	old

E X A M P L E : *I am outgoing.*

1. _____

   _____

2. _____

   _____

3. _____

   _____

4. _____

   _____

5. _____

   _____

Using the same list, write five sentences about your parents.

E X A M P L E : *My parents are happy.*

1. _____

_____

2. _____

_____

3. _____

_____

4. _____

_____

5. _____

_____

Using the same list, write five sentences about someone else in your family.

E X A M P L E : *My uncle is athletic.*

1. _____

_____

2. _____

_____

3. _____

_____

4. _____

_____

5. _____

_____

Exercise 4 *(Focus 1 and 2)*

PAIR

Share some of the sentences you wrote in Exercise 3 with a partner. Ask yes/no questions about the people your partner describes.

E X A M P L E : A: *My uncle is athletic.*

B: *Is he a basketball player?*

A: *No, he isn't. He is a tennis player.*

Exercise 5 *(Focus 3)*

Using the list of adjectives from Exercise 3, write five **negative statements** about yourself. Share the statements with your partner.

E X A M P L E :   *I'm not organized.*

1. _____
   _____

2. _____
   _____

3. _____
   _____

4. _____
   _____

5. _____
   _____

Exercise 6 *(Focus 3)*

Using the list of adjectives from Exercise 3 write five **negative statements** about people you know. Two of the sentences should be about two or more people.

E X A M P L E :   *Karen and Chet aren't talkative.*

1. _____
   _____

2. _____
   _____

3. _____
   _____

4. _____
   _____

5. _____
   _____

3

The Verb *Be*

Wh-Question

Exercise 1 *(Focus 1)*

Complete the story with the correct *Wh*-question word and the correct form of *be*. The firs
one has been done for you as an example.

Monte: Welcome to *The 64-Cent Question*, the game show where we ask easy questions and the contestants can win up to 64 cents. I'm your host, Monte Money, and our two contestants tonight are Feliz Happy and Sandy Beach. *How are* you tonight, Feliz?

Feliz: I'm just happy to be here, Monte.

Monte: Great, and (1) _____ _____ you Sandy?

Sandy: Fine, thank you, Monte.

Monte: Great, now let's begin tonight's game. The first question is for you, Feliz
(2) _____ _____ the capital of the United States?

Feliz: Washington, D.C.

Monte: Right! Now, for you Sandy. (3) _____ _____ the director of the movi
E.T.?

Sandy: Steven Spielberg.

Monte: Great! Now Feliz, (4) _____ _____ plants green?

Feliz: Because they contain chlorophyll.

Monte: You've got it. Sandy, (5) _____ old _____ the Great Pyramids in Egypt?

Sandy: About 4,700 years old.

Monte: Correct! Feliz, (6) _____ _____ the first day of spring?

Feliz: March 21st.

Monte: Right again! Now, Sandy, (7) _____ _____ Leonardo da Vinci's painting, the *Mona Lisa*?

Sandy: In the Louvre in Paris.

Monte: Yes! For you, Feliz, (8) _____ _____ 7 × 8?

Feliz: 56.

Monte: You're right again. Sandy, (9) _____ _____ the author of *Tom Sawyer*?

Sandy: Mark Twain.

Monte: Feliz, (10) _____ _____ the Statue of Liberty located?

Feliz: In New York.

Monte: Finally, for you Sandy, the last question. (11) _____ _____ Thanksgiving celebrated in the United States?

Sandy: On the third Thursday in November.

Monte: Amazing, folks! We have a tie! Well, tune in next week for *The 64-Cent Question*.

Exercise 2 *(Focus 2)*   PAIR

Look at this information while your partner looks at page 10. Your partner knows the meanings of five words and you know the meanings of five. Ask each other the definitions for each word and record them next to the words. Then answer your partner's questions about the words on your list.

1. banjo _____
2. talkative _____
3. lumberjack _____
4. fog _____
5. sailor _____

chubby: (adjective) Round and fat.

dye: (verb) To change the color.

hail: (noun) Small round pieces of frozen rain.

ignore: (verb) To pay no attention to.

pretend: (verb) To imagine; to make believe.

banjo: (noun) A musical instrument with a round body and five strings.

fog: (noun) Clouds that reach to the ground.

lumberjack: (noun) A person who cuts down trees.

sailor: (noun) A person who works on a boat.

talkative: (adjective) Talking a lot.

1. hail _____

2. pretend _____

3. ignore _____

4. chubby _____

5. dye _____

Exercise 3 *(Focus 3)*

Using the map below, answer the questions that follow.

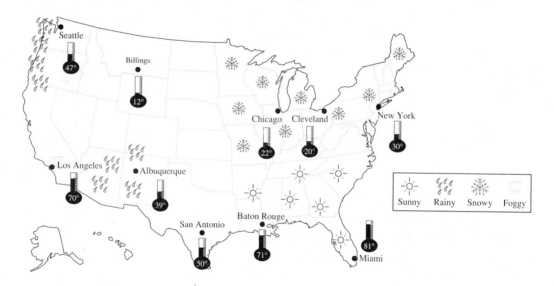

1. How's the weather in Miami today? _____

2. What's the temperature in Chicago? _____

3. How's the weather in Seattle? _____

4. What's the temperature in New York? _____

5. How's the weather in Los Angeles? _____

6. How's the weather in San Antonio? _____

7. What's the temperature in Cleveland? _____

8. How's the weather in Billings? _____

9. How's the weather in Albuquerque? _____

10. What's the temperature in Baton Rouge? _____

Exercise 4 *(Focus 3)*

Look in today's newspaper. Find the weather map. Ask your partner questions about the weather in different cities in the United States.

Exercise 5 *(Focus 4)*

Look at this map of the time zones of Asia. Answer the questions.

1. It's 7 A.M. in Bombay.
   What time is it in Calcutta? _____
2. It's 9 A.M. in Novosibirsk.
   What time is it in Beijing? _____
3. It's 11 A.M. in Phnom Penh.
   What time is it in Rangoon? _____
4. It's 10 A.M. in Ho Chi Minh City.
   What time is it in Bangkok? _____
5. It's 11 A.M. in Taipei.
   What time is it in Bangkok? _____

Number of hours to add to Greenwich time

+4.50		+6.50	
+5.00		+7.00	
+5.50		+8.00	
+5.66		+9.00	
+6.00		+10.00	

+4 +5 +6 +7 +8 +9 +10

Exercise 6 *(Focus 4)*

Write five more questions using the pattern from Exercise 5. Ask your partner the questions you wrote.

1. _____
2. _____
3. _____
4. _____
5. _____

Choose the <u>one</u> word or phrase that best completes the sentence.

1. The students _____ from Mexico.
   (A) and   (B) be
   (C) are   (D) is

2. When _____?
   (A) time is it   (B) is your vacation
   (C) is Canada   (D) old are you

3. _____ is married.
   (A) They   (B) It
   (C) We   (D) She

4. _____ students in level 1.
   (A) She is   (B) It is
   (C) They are   (D) I am

5. _____? It means very big.
   (A) What means huge   (B) What is the spelling of
                              huge
   (C) What is the meaning of   (D) What is the pronuncia-
       huge   tion of huge

6. _____ shy and athletic.
   (A) She's   (B) It isn't
   (C) Am   (D) It's

7. The student _____ Japanese.
   (A) is   (B) am
   (C) be   (D) she

8. _____ an English teacher.
   (A) They are   (B) I'm
   (C) They're   (D) To be

9. _____ Montreal? _____ in Quebec.
   (A) Where is . . . It's   (B) Where be . . . It is
   (C) Where is . . . Is   (D) When is . . . It's

10. Dr. Martin is _____.
    (A) opens   (B) busy
    (C) school   (D) yes

11. You_____ short.
    (A) it's   (B) am
    (C) no   (D) aren't

12. _____? I'm 35.
    (A) How age are you   (B) How are you
    (C) How old you are   (D) How old are you

13. _____ am not short.
    (A) I   (B) We're
    (C) She   (D) I'm

14. A: Hi! I'm Anne Parker.
    B:_____.
    (A) Nice to you meet, Ms.   (B) Nice to meet you, Ms.
           Parker   Anne
    (C) Is nice, Anne.   (D) Nice to meet you, Anne.

Identify the one underlined word or phrase that must be changed in order for the sentence to be grammatically correct.

15. Is it cold? What's the temperature today? It has 30 degrees.
        A   B   C   D

16. Is José from China? No, José's no from China.
        A   B   C D

17. Tense I am? Yes, you are; try to relax.
        A   B   C   D

18. Who is your teacher? Ms. Betty is my teacher.
        A   B   C   D

19. How are those problems? He isn't difficult.
        A   B   C   D

20. Are you single? Yes, I'm.
        A   B   C D

21. Is it raining? No, is not. It's sunny.
        A   B   C   D

22. What time it is? It's three o'clock Central time.
        A   B   C   D

23. How's the weather today? Is cool and rainy.
        A   B   C   D

24. When are you wet? I'm wet because of the rain.
        A   B   C   D

UNIT 4

Exercise 1 *(Focus 1)*

Grandma's shopping list

Butcher
pork chops
steak
hamburger
chicken

Produce Stand
potatoes
strawberries
carrots
onions
apple cider
broccoli
green beans

Dairy
milk
butter
ice cream

Bakery
brownies
rolls
doughnuts

Classify the foods on the shopping list as **count** or **non-count nouns.** The first one has been done for you as an example.

Count nouns

1. *Pork chops*
2. _____
3. _____
4. _____
5. _____
6. _____
7. _____
8. _____
9. _____
10. _____

Non-count nouns

1. _____
2. _____
3. _____
4. _____
5. _____
6. _____
7. _____

Exercise 2 (*Focus 2*)

Write the count nouns from the list in Exercise 1 in their **singular** form. Write *a* or *an* in front of the words.

1. _____   6. _____

2. _____   7. _____

3. _____   8. _____

4. _____   9. _____

5. _____   10. _____

Exercise 3 (*Focus 2*)

List all the words below in the correct categories. Write *a* or *an* in front of the words.

tie	month	potato	blouse	helicopter
day	carrot	airplane	radish	undershirt
pea	sweater	truck	sock	automobile
herb	year	week	train	hour

Clothes
1. _____
2. _____
3. _____
4. _____
5. _____

Transportation
1. _____
2. _____
3. _____
4. _____
5. _____

Vegetables
1. _____
2. _____
3. _____
4. _____
5. _____

Time
1. _____
2. _____
3. _____
4. _____
5. _____

Exercise 4 *(Focus 3)*

Complete the story with a **plural** form of the words below. The first one has been done fo
you.

house	witch	candy
princess	boy	holiday
girl	door	ax
cat	wish	hero
fairy	monster	knife
toy	country	orange
class	baby	trick
party	treat	story

Halloween in the United States

It is interesting to know about *holidays* in different (1) _____.
Halloween is celebrated on October 31 in the United States. Small children and even
(2) _____ wear costumes. Some children like frightening costumes.
They dress like (3) _____ and (4) _____. The
scary costumes can include plastic (5) _____ and (6) _____ with
fake blood, but they don't really hurt anyone. Some (7) _____ dress
like Superman and Batman and other (8) _____.
(9) _____ that give people (10) _____ or Cinderella, Sleeping Beauty, and other (11) _____ from (12) _____
are popular costumes for (13) _____. Still other children dress like
(14) _____ and other animals. In the afternoon the children have
(15) _____ in their (16) _____ at school. When it
gets dark, the children knock on the (17) _____ of all of the
(18) _____ in their neighborhood. The people in the houses give the
children (19) _____ like (20) _____, (21) _____
and other fruit, and small (22) _____. If they don't receive treats,
some children play (23) _____.

Exercise 5 *(Focus 4)*

Listen to your teacher read the **regular plural nouns** you used in Exercise 4. Write each word in the correct category according to its pronunciation. The first one has been done for you as an example.

/z/	/s/	/iz/
holidays		

Exercise 6 *(Focus 4)*

Practice saying each of the words in the lists you made in Exercise 5. Use a tape recorder if possible. Check your pronunciation.

Exercise 7 *(Focus 5)*

Write the **irregular plural** form of each of the following nouns in the correct category. Use a dictionary to look up words you do not know how to spell. The first one has been done for you as an example.

child	mouse
deer	ox
fish	person
foot	sheep
goose	tooth
man	moose
woman	

Humans	**Animals**	**Body Parts**
people		

17

Exercise 8 *(Focus 6)*

Circle the mistakes in the following paragraphs. Correct the mistakes and rewrite the paragraphs correctly. The first sentence has been done for you as an example.

Information(s are) easier to get with today's new technology. A news is transmitted around the world by TV satellites. Computers also make informations easier to get. Computers can help a person do his homeworks. Computer networks allow people to tell some news and give some advices. With computer mails, a person can send a message with an electricity and a phone line.

Information is easier to get with today's new technology.

_____

_____

_____

_____

_____

_____

_____

_____

_____

_____

_____

_____

_____

There is a new kind of store in the United States now. Superstores are a combination of supermarkets and discount stores. Superstores have everything from foods to furnitures. At a superstore you can buy beverages like a coffee, a tea, or a milk. In the same store you can buy jewelries, clothings, and coloring for your hairs. You can also buy things like a bread, a rice, a sugar, or a fruit. There is even a pharmacy where you can buy medicines. You should bring lots of monies with you when you go to a superstore because there is a lot to buy. But, one thing you can't buy at a superstore is the love.

_____

_____

_____

_____

_____

_____
_____
_____
_____
_____
_____
_____
_____
_____
_____
_____

Exercise 9 *(Focus 7)*

Look at picture A while your partner looks at picture B. You know some of the prices of the items for sale in the Gag-and-Save grocery store. Your partner knows the other prices. Take turns with your partner asking the prices of the missing items. Then switch pictures and ask each other more questions.

A   B

Exercise 10 *(Focus 7)*

Use the pictures from Exercise 9. Ask your partner more difficult questions by asking the price of more than one pound or item.

E X A M P L E :   *How much for two cans of peaches?*
$1.98.

UNIT

5

The Verb *Have*

Exercise 1 *(Focus 1)*

This is the Yohnson family from Wisconsin. Yan Yohnson, his wife Yill, and their son Yack have many things for the cold and snowy Wisconsin winters.

This is the Sunshine family from California. Ray Sunshine, his wife Tawny, and their daughter Malibu have many things for the warm California weather.

Using the words below, write sentences about what each family has.

E X A M P L E S :   sled: *Yack Yohnson has a sled.*
                house: *Both families have houses.*
                barbecue: *The Sunshine family has a barbecue.*

1. pet: _____
2. warm coat: _____
3. snow shovel: _____
4. hammock: _____
5. swimming pool: _____
6. porch: _____

7. children: _____

8. daughter: _____

9. son: _____

10. palm trees: _____

11. fireplace: _____

12. air conditioner: _____

13. woodpile: _____

14. scarf: _____

15. wife: _____

16. sunglasses: _____

Exercise 2 *(Focus 2)*

Use the pictures from Exercise 1. Complete the following sentences with true statements using the negative form of **have**.

E X A M P L E : Yan Yohnson *doesn't have a daughter.*

1. Ray Sunshine _____

2. The Yohnson family _____

3. Yan and Yill Yohnson _____

4. The Sunshines' house _____

5. Yack Yohnson _____

6. The dog _____

7. Malibu _____

8. The swimming pool _____

9. The cat _____

10. Tawny Sunshine _____

Exercise 3 (Focus 3)

Ask three classmates if they have the following items in their homes. Record their short answers on the chart below.

Do you have . . .	Name:	Name:	Name:
1. children?			
2. a tv?			
3. a car?			
4. a tent?			
5. a jet plane?			
6. a snow shovel?			
7. a watch?			
8. a sister?			
9. chopsticks?			
10. a swimming pool?			

Exercise 4 (Focus 3)

Write the questions that go with the following answers.

EXAMPLE: *Does Ray Sunshine have a son?*
No, he doesn't have a son.

1. _____

   Yes, they do have a swimming pool.

2. _____

   Yes, he does have a sled.

3. _____

   No, they don't have a fireplace.

4. _____

   Yes, she does have a cat.

5. _____

   Yes, they do have a fireplace.

6. _____

   No, they don't have a woodpile.

7. _____

Yes, California does have palm trees.

8. _____

No, Wisconsin doesn't have palm trees.

9. _____

Yes, they do have a hammock.

10. _____

Yes, Yack does have a warm coat.

11. _____

Yes, she does have sunglasses.

Exercise 5 *(Focus 4)*

Read the following questions. Check (✔) whether the speaker expects a positive response or is unsure of what the response will be.

	Positive	Unsure
EXAMPLE: Do you have any aspirin?	✔	—
1. I'm not sure what color to paint the bathroom. Do you have any advice?	—	—
2. This exercise is difficult. Can you give me some help?	—	—
3. My refrigerator just broke. Do you have any space in your refrigerator for this meat?	—	—
4. Does the library have any books about the Inuit people?	—	—
5. Do you have some extra paper I could borrow?	—	—

Exercise 6 *(Focus 4)*

Decide if either *some* or *any* is necessary in each blank in the dialogue below. Then write the correct word. If neither word is necessary, put an "*x*" in the blank. The first one has been done for you as an example.

Kay: What are you doing this weekend?

Ray: I don't know. I have <u>some</u> free time and I want to go to the movies, but I don't have (1) _____ money.

Kay: Doesn't your father have (2) _____ money that he could lend to you?

Ray: He has money, but he doesn't lend (3) _____ of it to me. He says that if I want (4) _____ money I have to work for it. I don't want to do (5) _____ work. I just want to have (6) _____ fun.

Kay: Working is not that hard. If you mow a couple of lawns you can make (7) _____ money fast.

Ray: I guess that isn't so difficult. Besides, I won't have (8) _____ fun if I stay home all weekend.

Exercise 7 *(Focus 5)*

Write the **polite request** for each cue.

E X A M P L E : books: *Excuse me, do you have any books?*

1. pencils: _____
2. telephone: _____
3. fountain pens: _____
4. basketballs: _____
5. restrooms: _____
6. photocopier: _____
7. Ashland University T-shirts: _____
8. notebooks: _____
9. computer disks: _____
10. comic books: _____

Exercise 8 *(Focus 5)*

Look at the picture of the Ashland University bookstore. Use the requests in Exercise 5. Take turns with your partner. Role-play a customer and a salesclerk in the book store. The salesclerk should answer the polite requests according to the picture.

Exercise 9 *(Focus 6)*

Use the pictures of the Yohnson and Sunshine families from Exercise 1. Write three sentences describing each person in the pictures. Use the verb *be* in one sentence in each group and *have* in two sentences.

EXAMPLE:　The Yohnsons

　　　　　　The Yohnsons are short.

　　　　　　The Yohnsons have black hair.

　　　　　　They have bangs.

Yan Yohnson

1. _____

2. _____

3. _____

Yill Yohnson

4. _____

5. _____

6. _____

Yack Yohnson

7. _____

8. _____

9. _____

The Sunshines

10. _____

11. _____

12. _____

Ray Sunshine

13. _____

14. _____

15. _____

Tawny Sunshine

16. _____

17. _____

18. _____

Malibu Sunshine

19. _____

20. _____

21. _____

UNIT

6

Possessives

Exercise 1 (*Focus 1*)

Choose the correct caption for each picture. Write its letter under the appropriate picture. The first one has been done for you as an example.

A. The secretaries' desks are messy.

B. Canada's flag has a maple leaf on it.

C. Erle's homework is incomplete.

D. Maya's car is a compact.

E. Mexico's flag has an eagle and a snake on it.

F. Mark's computer is new.

G. Monique's car is luxurious.

H. The secretaries' desks are neat.

I. James'computer is old.

J. Paulo's homework is finished.

1. <u>D</u>

2. —

3. —

4. —

5. —

6. —

7. ―

8. ―

9. ―

10. ―

Exercise 2 (Focus 2)

Write a sentence describing Marie's relationship with the people below.

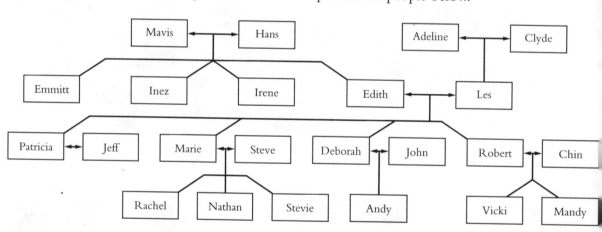

E X A M P L E : Nathan: *Nathan is Marie's son.*

1. Mandy: _____

2. Mavis: _____

3. Emmitt: _____

4. Steve: _____

5. Andy: _____

6. Les: _____

7. Rachel: _____

8. Stevie: _____

9. Hans: _____

10. Chin: _____

11. Jeff: _____

12. Adeline and Clyde: _____

13. Irene: _____

14. Vicki: _____

Exercise 3 (Focus 2)

Fill in the names in the blanks below to show your own family tree.

My Family Tree

_____	_____	_____	_____
Grandfather	Grandmother	Grandfather	Grandmother

_____	_____
Mother	Father

_____
Me

Answer the following questions about your family tree. Use complete sentences.

1. What is your mother's name?

   _____

2. What is your father's name?

   _____

3. What are your grandmothers' names?

   _____

4. What are your grandfathers' names?

   _____

Exercise 4 (Focus 3)

PAI

What are your three favorite possessions? List them and write an adjective that describes each possession. Then tell your partner about them.

E X A M P L E : *family photographs, priceless*

You say: *My family photographs are priceless.*

1. _____

2. _____

3. _____

Exercise 5 (Focus 3)

Tell the rest of your classmates about your partner's favorite possessions. Use **possessive adjectives**.

E X A M P L E : *Her family photographs are priceless.*

Exercise 6 (Focus 3)

Sun and Lee Park are brothers. They are from Korea. They are studying English in the United States, but they are studying in different schools and have different programs. Sun Park is studying at a community college. Lee is studying in the intensive language program at a university. The brothers talk to each other on the phone and compare the two different English programs.

Complete the dialogue using the correct **possessive adjectives**. The first one has been done for you as an example.

Sun: Hello, Lee. How are you? How is *your* English program?

Lee: It's great. I have small classes. (1) _____ classes only have 10 students.

Sun: That's good. (2) _____ classes are very crowded. I have 30 students in my classes.

Lee: Does (3) _____ program have a lab? We have a language lab. The lab has computers, tape recorders and listening stations.

Sun: Yes, we have several labs. The computer lab is very large and (4) _____ computers are all new.

Lee: What about your teacher?

Sun: She is very nice. (5) _____ name is Mrs. Nation. She always encourages us. She tells us (6) _____ English is improving every day.

Lee: (7) _____ teacher is a man. (8) _____ name is Mr. Bahamonde. He also encourages us, but (9) _____ tests are very difficult. He makes us work very hard. What about a text book? Which book are you using?

Sun: We're using *Grammar Dimensions*. It's a very good book and the activities are fun.

Lee: We're using *Grammar Dimensions* too. I like it. How much does (10) _____ program cost?

Sun: It's not too expensive.

Lee: (11) _____ program is expensive. The cost is high and I don't have any time to work.

Sun: You should try (12) _____ program; it is only part time.

Exercise 7 *(Focus 4)*

Find a person or persons in your class that fit the following descriptions, if you can. Write his/her/their name(s) in the boxes at the right. Complete the last five descriptions with your own words. Share your answers with your classmates.

Description	Names
1. Her eyes are dark.	
2. His legs are long.	
3. Their ears are small.	
4. His hair is long.	
5. Her waist is thin.	
6. Their hands are _____.	
7. Our arms are _____.	
8. My nose is _____.	
9. Our _____.	
10. My _____.	

Exercise 8 *(Focus 5)*

Match the people with their things. Then write a statement about the thing, using the correct possessive pronoun.

E X A M P L E : The calculator is hers.

Lucy is an accountant. —————————— a book bag
1. Billy is a truck driver. —————————————— a calculator
2. Rudolfo and Juan are   a cash register
   firemen.
3. Scott is a plumber.   a fire hose
4. Toni is a singer.   a dog leash
5. Joyce is a dog trainer.   police badges
6. Julia and Thomas are   plans for a house
   police officers.
7. Angie is a student.   music
8. Roy is a salesclerk.   a truck
9. Isaac is an architect.   a football
10. Bruce is a football player.   a wrench

1. _____

2. _____

3. _____

4. _____

5. _____

6. _____

7. _____

8. _____

9. _____

10. _____

Exercise 9 *(Focus 3, 5 and 6)*

Each object or person on the list below belongs to the people in the pictures. Using *whose*, ask questions to find out who the objects belong to. Make two statements, one with the **possessive noun** and one with the **possessive pronoun**.

E X A M P L E : *Whose false teeth are they? They're Joe's false teeth. They're his.*

Joe

Ashley

Ginette and Jasmine

1. mother _____

2. notebooks _____

3. boyfriends _____

4. rocking chair _____

5. false teeth _____

6. bottle _____

7. cane _____

8. tape players _____

9. toy _____

_____

10. cassette tapes _____

_____

11. glasses _____

_____

12. diaper _____

_____

Exercise 10 (Focus 7)

Choose the **indefinite** or **definite article** (*a*, *an*, or *the*) and fill in the blanks. The first one has been done for you as an example.

A Friend's Birthday

Cristina went to *a* bakery to buy a cake. (1) _____ bakery is new; it just opened last month. (2) _____ cake is for (3) _____ friend's birthday.

(4) _____ friend's name is Lola. She is from Colombia. This is the first birthday Lola is celebrating without her family. Cristina doesn't want Lola to feel bad because she isn't with her family.

Cristina wants to buy Lola (5) _____ special present. But (6) _____ present can't cost too much because Cristina doesn't have much money. Cristina looks for (7) _____ umbrella. She thinks that (8) _____ umbrella will make (9) _____ practical and beautiful gift.

When she finds (10) _____ perfect umbrella she tries to wrap it in colorful paper, but (11) _____ umbrella is (12) _____ difficult present to wrap. Finally, she just puts (13) _____ big bow on (14) _____ umbrella.

When Cristina gives Lola (15) _____ present and (16) _____ cake, she is surprised. She is happy to have (17) _____ good friend like Cristina.

TOEFL® Test Preparation
Exercises · Units 4–6

Choose the <u>one</u> word or phrase that best completes the sentence.

1. The teacher _____ problem.
   - (A) has a
   - (B) has any
   - (C) be a
   - (D) have any

2. They _____ have computers at that school.
   - (A) doesn't
   - (B) aren't
   - (C) don't
   - (D) no

3. What's that? It's _____ airplane.
   - (A) any
   - (B) a
   - (C) an
   - (D) some

4. She doesn't _____ new book.
   - (A) has a
   - (B) have an
   - (C) has an
   - (D) have a

5. Costa Rica and Brazil are _____.
   - (A) countrys
   - (B) a country
   - (C) country
   - (D) countries

6. I _____ children.
   - (A) no have any
   - (B) don't have some
   - (C) don't have any
   - (D) doesn't has any

7. He has _____ homework.
   - (A) a
   - (B) one
   - (C) any
   - (D) some

8. Do the children _____ toys? The _____ are new.
   - (A) has any . . . children's toys
   - (B) have any . . . childrens' toys
   - (C) has a . . . children's toy
   - (D) have any . . . children's toys

9. Ulrika _____ children.
   - (A) has one
   - (B) has two
   - (C) have some
   - (D) have any

10. They _____ bread.
    - (A) have a
    - (B) has some
    - (C) have any
    - (D) have some

11. She _____ short, brown hair.

    (A) no has   (B) doesn't have

    (C) doesn't has   (D) don't has

12. There are two _____.

    (A) deer   (B) deers

    (C) mans   (D) man

13. I have _____ sugar in the cupboard. There isn't _____ more in the bowl.

    (A) some . . . any   (B) some . . . some

    (C) a . . . any   (D) a . . . some

14. Do the dogs have food? No, the _____ are empty.

    (A) dog's bowls   (B) dogs' bowls

    (C) dog's bowl   (D) dogs' bowl

15. The cat has a bed. _____ bed is comfortable.

    (A) It's   (B) Its

    (C) Your   (D) Their

Identify the one underlined word or phrase that must be changed in order for the sentence to be grammatically correct.

16. Mickey is a famous mice in the Florida attraction, Disney World.
           A B   C   D

17. Do you have three watchs on your wrist?
    A   B   C   D

18. My house have heat in all of the rooms except the garage.
    A   B   C   D

19. How many does a hamburger cost at that new restaurant in Orlando?
    A   B   C   D

20. I have a daughter. My daughter's hair is black like my.
    A   B   C   D

21. The coffee is hot. Her wants to drink some after she finishes her dinner.
    A   B   C   D

22. Who paper is this? It has Joan's name on it. I think it is hers.
     A   B   C   D

23. Luzmilla doesn't have a book. Please, give the new English book to she. It is hers.
           A   B C D

24. Whose homeworks are on the table? I think it's Sancho's homework.
    A   B   C

    He doesn't have his.
          D

25. Do you have any biographies? Yes, we have many books about the lifes of famou
    A   B   C

    people.
    D

Demonstratives

Exercise 1 *(Focus 1)*

Look at the pages from the two different catalogs. Complete the sentences below using the correct **demonstrative pronouns** and the correct form of the verb *be*.

EXAMPLE: *Those are* shoes.

1. _____ a beret.
2. _____ a thick sweater.
3. _____ a cowboy hat.
4. _____ shorts.
5. _____ a polka-dot dress.
6. _____ shoes.
7. _____ an expensive sweater.
8. _____ long pants.
9. _____ a necklace.
10. _____ a bracelet.
11. _____ a striped shirt.

Exercise 2 *(Focus 2)*

Rewrite the sentences from Exercise 1 using **demonstrative adjectives**.

E X A M P L E : *Those shoes are black.*

1. _____
2. _____
3. _____
4. _____
5. _____
6. _____
7. _____
8. _____
9. _____
10. _____
11. _____

Exercise 3 *(Focus 3)*

Lucia is looking at pictures of Paul's family. Using the cues in the picture, complete her *yes/no* questions with the correct form of the verb *be* and a **demonstrative**. Then complete Paul's short answer. The first one is done for you as an example.

38

Lucia	Paul
Is this your mother?	Yes, *it is*.
1. _____ _____ your brothers?	No, _____ _____.
	They're my cousins.
2. _____ _____ your sister?	Yes, _____ _____.
3. _____ _____ her dog?	Yes, _____ _____.
4. _____ _____ your father?	Yes, _____ _____.
5. _____ _____ his boat?	No, _____ _____.
	It's a neighbor's boat.
6. _____ _____ your parents in the wedding picture?	Yes, _____ _____.
7. _____ _____ a real diamond necklace?	No, _____ _____.
8. _____ _____ you when you were a baby?	Yes, _____ _____.
9. _____ _____ your girlfriend?	No, _____ _____.
	I don't have a girlfriend.

Exercise 4 *(Focus 4)*

Write questions using demonstratives for the nouns below. Then answer the questions. Use the words in the list below as cues.

E X A M P L E : close: newspapers, magazines *What are these? These are things to read.*

things to read	toy	types of transportation	furniture
kitchen machines	trees	flower	bedding
places to live	meat	colors	

1. far: couch, bed _____
2. close: chicken, beef _____
3. far: doll _____
4. close: car, motorcycle _____
5. far: green, yellow _____
6. close: pine, maple _____
7. close: daisy _____
8. far: apartment, house _____
9. close: can opener, toaster _____
10. close: blanket, sheet _____

UNIT

8

Be + Prepositional Phrase,
Where Questions

Exercise 1 (Focus 1)

Read the directions carefully. Draw the figures according to the directions. Then write
sentence about each figure you draw using the verb *be* and a **prepositional phrase**. The firs
one has been done for you as an example.

1. Draw a square.
2. Draw a triangle above the square.
3. Draw two rectangles under the square.
4. Draw a face on the square.
5. Draw a circle beside the square.

1. *The square is under the triangle*
2. _____
3. _____
4. _____
5. _____

6. Draw a circle.
7. Draw another circle next to the first circle.
8. Draw a line between the circles.
9. Draw a square in front of the circles.
10. Draw two triangles above each circle.

6. _____
7. _____
8. _____
9. _____
10. _____

11. Draw a man.
12. Draw a woman beside the man.
13. Draw a boy in front of the man.
14. Draw a girl between the man and the woman.
15. Draw a house in back of the people.

11. _____
12. _____
13. _____
14. _____
15. _____

Exercise 2 *(Focus 1)*

Draw a simple picture, but don't show it to your partner. Tell your partner how to draw the picture using the verb *be* and **prepositional phrases**.

Exercise 3 *(Focus 2)*

Using *where are* or *where is*, write a question. Then answer your questions according to the picture. Don't use *on the floor* or *on the dresser* more than once.

E X A M P L E :   towels: *Where are the towels? On the dresser.*

1. keys: _____
2. shirt: _____
3. pants: _____
4. books: _____
5. shoes: _____
6. sweater: _____
7. jewelry: _____
8. glasses: _____
9. pillow: _____
10. brush: _____
11. jacket: _____

Intensifiers

Exercise 1 *(Focus 1)*

Think about the following subjects. Rate them on the continuum using the adjectives provided. Then write two sentences, one positive and one negative. Use an **intensifier** in each
sentence.

E X A M P L E : **Speaking English**

difficult ——————————————————— X ——————————— easy

Speaking English is fairly easy.

It isn't very difficult.

1. **Studying Chemistry**

   difficult ——————————————————————————————————————— easy

   _____

   _____

2. **A Rolls Royce**

   elegant ——————————————————————————————————————— plain

   _____

   _____

3. **Horror Films**

   frightening ——————————————————————————————————— funny

   _____

   _____

4. **Antarctica**

   warm ——— cold

   _____

   _____

5. **The Mediterranean Sea**

   clean ——————————————————————————————————————— polluted

   _____

   _____

6. Moscow, Russia

large ———————————————————————————— small

——————————————————————————————————————

——————————————————————————————————————

7. Airplanes

loud ———————————————————————————— quiet

——————————————————————————————————————

——————————————————————————————————————

Exercise 2 *(Focus 2)*

Dream Date

Grace wants her friend Charlene to go on a blind date (a date with someone she doesn't know). Charlene wants to find out more information about the person. Use the cues to write the questions Charlene will ask Grace about the person Grace wants her to date.

E X A M P L E : eyes: *What are his eyes like?*

1. hair: ————————————————————————————————

2. family: ——————————————————————————————

3. clothes: —————————————————————————————

4. dancing: —————————————————————————————

5. manners: —————————————————————————————

6. apartment: ————————————————————————————

7. personality: ———————————————————————————

8. car: ——————————————————————————————————

Exercise 3 *(Focus 2)*

Below are parts of the answers Grace gives Charlene. But Charlene wants more specific information. Write the how question Charlene asks to get more information.

E X A M P L E : blue: *How blue are his eyes?*

1. dark: ——————————————————————————————————

2. rich: ——————————————————————————————————

3. expensive: ————————————————————————————

4. graceful: —————————————————————————————

5. polite: ————————————————————————————————

6. large: ——————————————————————————————————

7. friendly: —————————————————————————————

8. fast: ——————————————————————————————————

Exercise 4 *(Focus 3)*

Write a complete sentence describing the following nouns. Use an **adjective** before each noun.

EXAMPLE: your favorite sport: *Soccer is an exciting sport.*

1. your favorite sport: _____
2. your school: _____
3. your favorite type of music: _____
4. your favorite dessert: _____
5. your friend: _____
6. your favorite book: _____
7. your job: _____
8. your boss: _____
9. your teacher: _____
10. your native country: _____

Exercise 5 *(Focus 3)*

Rewrite the sentences from Exercise 4 with an **intensifier**.

EXAMPLE: *Soccer is a very exciting sport.*

1. _____
2. _____
3. _____
4. _____
5. _____
6. _____
7. _____
8. _____
9. _____
10. _____

Choose the <u>one</u> word or phrase that best completes the sentence.

1. Where are the dishes? They're _____ the cupboard _____ the stove.
   (A) in . . . above
   (B) on . . . inside
   (C) above . . . between
   (D) in front . . . on

2. The mug is _____ new.
   (A) fairly
   (B) near
   (C) this
   (D) every

3. _____ a can.
   (A) Is
   (B) They're
   (C) This
   (D) That's

4. Mary's desk is _____ large.
   (A) on
   (B) useful
   (C) quite
   (D) hers

5. _____? They're on the coffee table.
   (A) Where my books
   (B) Where are my books
   (C) Are where my books
   (D) Where my books are

6. Give me _____ paints.
   (A) every
   (B) that
   (C) ones
   (D) those

7. The car isn't _____ expensive.
   (A) pretty
   (B) fairly
   (C) quite
   (D) very

8. This is a _____.
   (A) shoes
   (B) that
   (C) chair
   (D) homework

9. The parking lot is _____ the store.
   (A) between
   (B) in back
   (C) near of
   (D) in back of

10. Who _____?
    (A) is they
    (B) are they
    (C) are he
    (D) are there

11. What's _____? _____ a popsicle.
    (A) these . . . They're   (B) that . . . They're
    (C) this . . . It's   (D) those . . . They're

12. That is my house, _____ the park and the drug store.
    (A) between   (B) near of
    (C) in front   (D) beside of

13. _____ mixed nuts?
    (A) Is that   (B) Are these
    (C) These   (D) That

14. The souvenir shop is _____ our hotel.
    (A) between   (B) opposite
    (C) close   (D) in back

15. _____ is your house? It's _____ big. It has four bedrooms.
    (A) How . . . pretty   (B) How big . . . not fairly
    (C) How big . . . quite   (D) How . . . not very

Identify the one underlined word or phrase that must be changed in order for the sentence to be grammatically correct.

16. Chicago is <u>on Lake Michigan</u>. The Sears Tower and the John Hancock building <u>are</u>
                  A   **B**
    <u>tall very</u> buildings <u>in Chicago</u>.
    C   **D**

17. <u>Where</u> the <u>children are</u>? They're <u>in</u> <u>that</u> store.
    A   **B**   **C**   **D**

18. <u>What's this</u>? <u>They're</u> fruit for the party. <u>There's an apple</u> for you in the <u>refrigerator</u>.
    A   **B**   **C**   **D**

19. <u>Those gum</u> is <u>pretty</u> old. It tastes <u>rather stale</u>. <u>This gum</u> is fresh.
    A   **B**   **C**   **D**

20. A house <u>near the country club</u> is <u>quite expensive</u>, but a house <u>in back of the airport</u>
              A   **B**   **C**
    <u>isn't quite expensive</u>.
    D

21. <u>Opposite of the bakery</u> there is a new store. <u>That store</u> is <u>open</u> <u>now</u>.
    A   **B**   **C**   **D**

22. I hope I like <u>this party</u>. <u>Are</u> <u>that people</u> friendly? I'm <u>somewhat shy</u> in new situations.
            A   **B**   **C**   **D**

23. <u>Are those</u> my clothes here? No, they aren't. <u>Yours</u> are <u>on</u> the <u>dresser</u>.
    A   **B**   **C**   **D**

24. What are <u>those things</u> between the <u>bananas and the apples</u>? <u>They're</u> plantains. <u>Are</u> deli-
            A   **B**   **C**   **D**
    cious.

25. <u>These shoes</u> hurt my feet. <u>Their</u> too small. I think <u>those shoes</u> <u>on the shelf</u> will fit better.
    A   **B**   **C**   **D**

There + Be

Exercise 1 *(Focus 1)*

Look at the picture of Farmer Dell's farm. Circle the sentence in each pair that best describes this picture.

DUANE GILLOGLY

E X A M P L E : A farm is in the picture.   (There is a farm in this picture.)

1. There is a pig.   A pig is in the picture.
2. A horse is in the barn.   There is a horse in the barn.
3. Chickens are in the chicken coop.   There are chickens in the chicken coop.
4. There is hay in the barn.   Hay is in the barn.
5. The goat is beside the barn.   There's a goat beside the barn.
6. The farmer is in his truck.   There's a farmer in the truck.
7. There are ducks on the pond.   Ducks are on the pond.
8. There is a rooster on the chicken coop.   A rooster is on the chicken coop.
9. There is corn in the field.   Some corn is in the field.
10. Two cows are in the barn.   There are two cows in the barn.

Exercise 2 (Focus 2)

Farmer McDonald has some problems on his farm. There are twelve things wrong wit[h] this picture. Write **affirmative statements** about the picture with *there + be*, using the cue[s] below.

EXAMPLE: horse: *There is a horse on the roof.*

1. pig: _____
2. chickens: _____
3. corn: _____
4. goat, duck, rooster: _____
5. TV: _____
6. electricity: _____
7. cows: _____
8. hat: _____
9. glasses: _____
10. dog: _____
11. furniture: _____

Exercise 3 (Focus 3)

Cecelia is choosing a college to study at. She likes the academic program and teachers at New College, but she wants to have more services and facilities. Cecelia made a list of things New College doesn't have. Change the list into **negative statements** using *there + be*.

E X A M P L E : smoking area in the cafeteria: *There's no smoking area in the cafeteria.*

1. swimming pool: _____
2. job counselors: _____
3. college radio station: _____
4. public transportation to town: _____
5. cultural events: _____
6. golf course: _____
7. math tutor: _____
8. drug store close to the campus: _____
9. quiet places to study: _____
10. soccer team: _____

Exercise 4 (Focus 4)

Imagine that you are trying to choose a school or college. Using the cues, write questions about the services and facilities available at a school.

E X A M P L E : job counselors: *Are there any job counselors?*

1. academic counselors: _____
2. library: _____
3. scholarships: _____
4. financial aid money: _____
5. sports teams: _____
6. bookstore: _____
7. student clubs: _____
8. tutors: _____
9. dorms: _____
10. entertainment: _____

Simple Present Tense

Exercise 1 *(Focus 1)*

Choose the correct word in parentheses to complete the story. Be careful to make the subject and verb agree. The first one has been done for you as an example.

I *want* (want, wants) you to meet my friend Herb Ban
and his wife, Sunny. They (1) _____ (live, lives)
in the city. Herb (2) _____ (like, likes) the city because his apartment is close to his job. Herb (3) _____
(walk, walks) to work every morning. He (4) _____
(work, works) in the building across the street from his
apartment. In the winter, Herb (5) _____ (go, goes)
to work without getting cold. He just
(6) _____ (walk, walks) through a tunnel that (7) _____ (go, goes) between
the two buildings.

Sunny, Herb's wife, (8) _____ (think, thinks) the city is all right, but she
(9) _____ (prefer, prefers) the country. Sunny (10) _____ (enjoy, enjoys) camping in the mountains. Every summer, they (11) _____ (camp, camps) in Montana for
two weeks. Herb always (12) _____ (complain, complains) about the mosquitoes.
He (13) _____ (hate, hates) mosquitoes.

Personally, I (14) _____ (want, wants) to live in the country, but I'm like Herb. I
(15) _____ (work, works) in the city.

Exercise 2 *(Focus 2)*

Thad Thrifty always tries to save money and resources. Before he goes grocery shopping, he checks the advertisements in the newspaper and cuts coupons to save money. When he washes clothes, he uses cold water to save energy. He also dries his clothes outside on a clothesline when the weather is nice. He conserves electricity when possible. He always turns off lights when he leaves a room.

Cara Careless spends money all the time. She buys food because it looks tasty. She forgets to plan meals so she eats out a lot. She wastes water when she washes her car. She always forgets to turn off her stereo when she leaves the house. She always dries her clothes in the dryer, even when the weather is warm.

Using the cues below make true statements about the habits and routines of Thad and Cara.

E X A M P L E : check advertisements: *Chad checks advertisements.*

1. waste water: _____

2. use a clothesline: _____

3. save coupons: _____

4. forget to turn off stereo: _____

   _____

5. eat out a lot: _____

6. save energy: _____

7. use cold water to wash clothes: _____

   _____

8. dry clothes in a dryer: _____

9. buy food because it looks tasty: _____

10. turn off lights: _____

11. try to save money: _____

12. spend money all the time: _____

Exercise 3 (Focus 2)

Do you try to save money and energy? Check the statements below that are generally tru
for you. Compare your answers with your partner. Who is more thrifty?

— I check advertisements for sales on food or clothes.

— I save coupons.

— I read labels carefully before I buy something.

— I plan my meals.

— I conserve water.

— I wash my clothes in cold water.

— I dry my clothes on a clothesline.

— I eat at restaurants most of the time.

— I waste water when brushing my teeth.

— I forget to turn off lights when I leave the room.

— I always dry my clothes in a dryer.

Exercise 4 (Focus 3)

Using the cues, make true statements about yourself by adding a **time expression** at the en
or beginning of the sentence. Skip the statements that are not true for you.

EXAMPLE: go to school: *I go to school three days a week.*

1. go to school: _____

2. eat pizza: _____

3. see your family: _____

4. drink wine: _____

5. call your mother: _____

6. cook a meal: _____

7. watch TV: _____

8. go to the dentist: _____

9. eat Chinese food: _____

10. wash your clothes: _____

11. pay your bills: _____

12. read the newspaper: _____

Exercise 5 *(Focus 4)*

Write statements about your partner using 10 of the verbs below. Read the statements to your partner. Try to pronounce each verb correctly in the **third person singular.** If possible, record yourself and listen to your pronunciation.

make	clean	wash	work	iron	rush	walk
fight	run	fix	sleep	swim	mix	read
watch	help	freeze	eat	like	wish	cook

1. _____
2. _____
3. _____
4. _____
5. _____
6. _____
7. _____
8. _____
9. _____
10. _____

Exercise 6 *(Focus 4)*

Finish the story with the correct form of the verb in parentheses. Be careful of irregular spelling. Then read the story out loud. If possible, record yourself and listen for the correct pronunciation of the verbs. The first one has been done for you as an example.

Norman *goes* (go) to work on the bus. He (1) _____ (hurry) to the bus stop because he doesn't want to miss the bus. Norman (2) _____ (enjoy) his work, but he (3) _____ (worry) when he is late. His boss (4) _____ (have) strict rules about being on time.

Norman (5) _____ (work) for a toy company. He (6) _____ (test) toys. Every morning Norman (7) _____ (have) a box of new toys on his desk. First, he (8) _____ (empty) the box and (9) _____ (look) at the toys he will test. Then, Norman (10) _____ (play) with the toys. He (11) _____ (try) them out.

After he (12) _____ (see) what a toy (13) _____ (do), Norman (14) _____ (write) a report about the toy. The report (15) _____ (say) what age child the toy is best for. It also (16) _____ (tell) about any possible dangers to children. Then Norman (17) _____ (send) his report and the toy to his boss.

Exercise 7 (Focus 5)

Make a list of things that you usually do in each of the following time periods. Then writ
sentences about your activities using *in, at,* or *on.*

EXAMPLE: **summer**

take a vacation: In the summer, I take a vacation.

go camping: I go camping in the summer.

summer

1. _____

2. _____

3. _____

Mondays

4. _____

5. _____

6. _____

noon

7. _____

8. _____

9. _____

weekends

10. _____

11. _____

12. _____

December

13. _____

14. _____

15. _____

Exercise 8 (Focus 5)

Ask your partner the following questions. Use the information in Exercise 7 to help you with your answers.

EXAMPLE: A: *What do you usually do in the summer?*
B: *I usually take a vacation. I usually go camping in the summer.*

1. What do you usually do in the summer?
2. What do you usually do on Mondays?
3. What do you usually do at noon?
4. What do you usually do on weekends?
5. What do you usually do in December?

Exercise 9 (Focus 6)

Don and Ron are brothers. They are different in some ways and the same in others. Look at the information about Don and Ron. Using the cues, make negative sentences.

Don is an accountant; he works in a big office downtown. He has a sports car and lives in an apartment. Still, Don likes to stay healthy. He likes exercise, but he doesn't like jogging. He enjoys playing basketball with his friends. He likes to do active things—he doesn't like going to movies. He is a vegetarian, and he doesn't smoke.

Ron is a park ranger; he works outdoors. He has a pickup truck and lives in a house. Ron likes to stay healthy. He likes exercise, but he doesn't like jogging. He prefers playing volleyball with his friends. Ron doesn't like basketball or movies. He doesn't smoke and he is a vegetarian.

EXAMPLES: work outside: *Don doesn't work outside.*
eat meat: *Don and Ron don't eat meat.*

1. work inside: _____
2. live in a house: _____
3. smoke: _____
4. have a sports car: _____
5. play volleyball: _____

6. jog: _____

7. like team sports: _____

8. drive a pickup truck: _____

9. live in an apartment: _____

10. like movies: _____

11. like basketball: _____

12. eat meat: _____

Exercise 10 (*Focus 7*)

Read the list of activities below. Do good parents do these things? Check **yes** or **no**. Then
write a statement about each, making it affirmative or negative. The first one has been done
for you as an example.

	Yes	No
let their children stay up late every night *Good parents don't let their children stay up late every night.*	____	✓

1. let their children play in the street

   _____

2. make their children do chores (household jobs)

   _____

3. give their children an allowance (weekly money)

   _____

4. let their children watch TV five hours every day

   _____

5. leave their children at home alone

   _____

6. give their children cigarettes

   _____

7. feed their children healthy food

   _____

8. help their children with their homework   ——   ——

_____

_____

9. let their children go to the library   ——   ——

_____

_____

10. buy their children bicycles   ——   ——

_____

Exercise 11 *(Focus 8)*

Write a *go*-expression to solve each of the following problems. The first one has been done for you as an example.

Problem	Solution
You are bored.	*Go to the movies.*
You need exercise.	1. _____
You want to see your family.	2. _____
You want an education.	3. _____
You want to see the ocean.	4. _____
You need some new clothes.	5. _____
You need a stamp.	6. _____
You have a toothache.	7. _____
You like winter sports.	8. _____
You need some money.	9. _____
You have the flu.	10. _____
You are tired.	11. _____
You are hungry.	12. _____
You want to see some natural beauty.	13. _____
You want to eat fish for dinner.	14. _____

Exercise 12 *(Focus 9)*

Complete the story with the correct form of *make* or *do*. The first one has been done for you as an example.

My schedule is different from most people's because I work at night. I wake up at noon and *make* my bed and (1)_____ some exercises. Then, I (2) _____ lunch. Usually I (3) _____ myself a sandwich.

After lunch, I go to college to study engineering because I want to get a better job. I always (4) _____ my homework right after class.

My wife, Gloria, (5) _____ me some dinner. I eat it after I finish my homework.

At six, I go to work. I am a telephone ticket agent for a big airline. When someone (6) _____ a request for a flight, I (7) _____ a reservation for them. I also help people (8) _____ plans for their vacations. I work until 3 A.M. When I come home I (9) _____ myself some breakfast.

During the week, Gloria (10) _____ most of the housework. She (11) _____ the laundry and the dishes. But on the weekends I help too. I (12) _____ the shopping and help with the cleaning.

Simple Present Tense

Exercise 1 *(Focus 1)*

Using the cues, write *yes/no* questions. Then ask your partner the questions. Record his or her short answers.

EXAMPLE: watch sports on TV

Do you watch sports on TV?

Yes, I do. or *No, I don't.*

Name: _____

1. watch sports on TV _____
2. sing in the shower _____
3. work _____
4. have a hobby _____
5. believe in ghosts _____
6. cook your own meals _____
7. like to dance _____
8. take vacations _____
9. have a pet _____
10. play chess _____

Exercise 2 *(Focus 1)*

Change partners. Ask your new partner about his or her first partner. Use the same cues as in Exercise 1. Record your new partner's short answers about his or her old partner.

EXAMPLE: *Does Mohammad watch sports on TV? Yes, he does.*

Name: _____

1. watch sports on TV _____
2. sing in the shower _____
3. work _____
4. have a hobby _____
5. believe in ghosts _____

6. cook his or her own meals _____

7. like to dance _____

8. take vacations _____

9. have a pet _____

10. play chess _____

Exercise 3 *(Focus 2)*

The chart below shows healthy and unhealthy habits and **adverbs of frequency**. Check th box that is true for you.

Adverbs of Frequency

Habits	Always	Almost always	Usually; Generally	Often; Frequently	Sometimes	Seldom; Rarely	Never
1. exercise							
2. eat fresh vegetables							
3. sleep eight hours							
4. relax							
5. drink water							
6. take vitamins							
7. eat junk food							
8. drink alcohol							
9. drive too fast							
10. smoke cigarettes							
11. get sunburned							

Exercise 4 *(Focus 3)*

Using your answers from Exercise 3, write sentences about your healthy or unhealthy habits. Compare your answers with your classmates. Who has healthy habits? Who has unhealthy habits?

EXAMPLE: *I frequently exercise.*

1. _____
2. _____
3. _____
4. _____
5. _____
6. _____
7. _____
8. _____
9. _____
10. _____
11. _____

Exercise 5 *(Focus 4)*

Fanny Fad, a reporter for *Teen Star* magazine interviewed these teenage stars. Read Fanny's article about each star. Then finish the questions Fanny asked using the cues.

Chris Crash 15

Chris Crash is an actor who likes to skateboard. He likes skateboarding because it is a fast sport. Chris lives in California. He practices skateboarding every day after school. He learns new skateboard tricks by studying other skateboarders. Chris wants to act in a skateboard movie.

Fanny's Questions to Chris

EXAMPLE: What *do you like to do?*

1. Why _____
2. Where _____
3. How often _____
4. When _____
5. How _____
6. What _____

Suzy Flex, 12

Suzy likes gymnastics. She practices hard because she wants to compete in the summer Olympics. She rehearses her gymnastic routines twice a day at the gym. She practices at 5:00 every morning and 4:30 every afternoon. She learns new routines with the help of her coach.

Fanny's Questions to Suzy

7. What _____

8. Why _____

9. How often _____

10. Where _____

11. What time _____

12. How _____

Exercise 6 *(Focus 4)*

Write the *Wh*-question that goes with each of the answers.

E X A M P L E : *Where does your mother live?*
          My mother lives in Brazil.

1. _____

   I call my parents once a week on Saturday.

2. _____

   My parents wait for my call.

3. _____

   They wait because they know I will always call on time.

4. _____

   I call at 8 P.M.

5. _____

   My brother lives in Brazil also.

6. _____

   He is a clerk in a government office.

7. _____

   He works in Brasilia.

8. _____

   My parents live in São Paulo.

9. _____

   He lives in Brasilia because it is the capital of Brazil.

10. _____

   My brother goes to São Paulo on holidays.

Exercise 7 *(Focus 5)*

Answer the questions below according to the picture of Breeze Port.

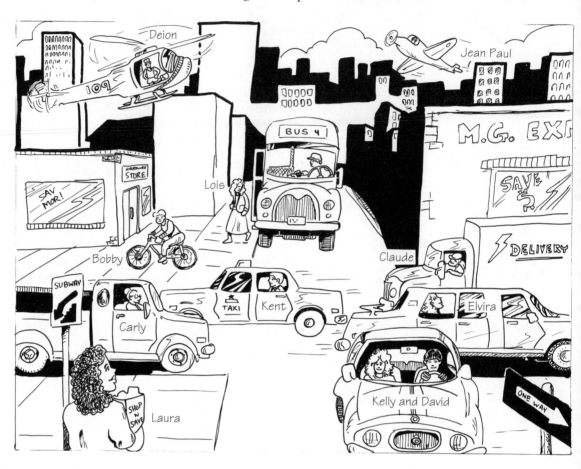

EXAMPLE: How does Bobby get to school? *by bike*

1. How does Elvira get to the theater? _____

2. How does Jean Paul get to Breeze Port? _____

3. How do Kelly and David get to work? _____

4. How does Carly get to work? _____

5. How does Deion get to the stadium? _____

6. How does Claude get to work? _____

7. How does Kent get to his office? _____

8. How does Lois get to work? _____

9. How does Laura go shopping? _____

Exercise 8 *(Focus 6)*

Read the story. Write *who* or *whom* questions to go with each answer.

Jill, Mandy, and Joy are roommates. They share an apartment near the college where they go to school. They share the responsibilities for the apartment and they also do many things together.

Jill drives Mandy and Joy to school every day. Joy makes dinner on weekdays and Mandy makes dinner on weekends. Joy's responsibility is to take out the trash on Mondays. Mandy puts out the recycling on Wednesdays. Jill washes her car on Saturdays.

Usually their friends, Sam, Roy, and George, eat dinner with them on Saturdays. Mandy and Jill also play tennis together.

EXAMPLE: *Who are Mandy's roommates?*

Jill and Joy are Mandy's roommates.

1. _____

   Mandy and Jill share an apartment with Joy.

2. _____

   Mandy, Jill, and Joy go to school.

3. _____

   Jill drives the car.

4. _____

   Mandy and Joy ride with Jill.

5. _____

   Joy cooks dinner on Tuesdays.

6. _____

   Mandy prepares dinner on the weekends.

7. _____

   Joy takes out the trash.

8. _____

   Mandy puts out the recycling.

9. _____

   Jill washes her own car.

10. _____

    They eat with Sam, George, and Roy on Saturday nights.

11. _____

    Mandy and Jill play tennis.

12. _____

    Jill plays tennis with Mandy.

Exercise 9 (*Focus 7*)

Read the following questions. Write *I* in front of the question if it is **informal.** Write *F* in front of the question if it is **formal.**

EXAMPLE: <u>F</u> With whom will you be attending the party?

___ 1. Who will you give the flowers to?

___ 2. To whom do you give your loyalty?

___ 3. For whom is this package?

___ 4. Who has my new hair dryer?

___ 5. Who wants ice cream?

___ 6. Who studies on weekends?

___ 7. With whom do you play tennis?

___ 8. Who sings the duet with you?

Exercise 10 (*Focus 8*)

Read each question. If it is correct write *C* in front of it. If it is incorrect write *I* in front of it and rewrite the question correctly.

EXAMPLE: <u>I</u> How you pronounce toothache?
How do you pronounce toothache.

___ 1. How do you spell *sincerely?*

_____

___ 2. How you say the opposite of *tired?*

_____

___ 3. How to pronounce *potato?*

_____

___ 4. What means *illogical?*

_____

___ 5. What the word *frantic* means?

_____

___ 6. How do you say the opposite of *freedom?*

_____

___ **7.** How spell *Wednesday?*

_____

___ **8.** How you pronounce your name?

_____

___ **9.** What do means *ethical.*

_____

___ **10.** How you say *a little wet?*

_____

Exercise 11 *(Focus 8)*

Using the appropriate question, ask your partner about the things below. If neither of you knows the correct answer, look it up in a dictionary.

E X A M P L E :   Q: *What is the opposite of boring?*
A: *Interesting.*

Opposites	Spelling	Pronunciation
boring	your name	through
relaxed	Mississippi	Illinois
winter	caution	your name

Meaning	Description
neither	a thing that a baby drinks from
upset	the square thing you put into a computer
obligatory	a chair with no back—only legs

Choose the <u>one</u> word or phrase that best completes the sentence.

1. _____ live in Baltimore?
   - (A) Do she
   - (B) Do you
   - (C) Does they
   - (D) Do he

2. Carmela gets home _____ 5:00 and prepares dinner.
   - (A) at
   - (B) in
   - (C) on
   - (D) to

3. Do you _____ work on Saturday? Yes, I _____ work on Saturdays.
   - (A) usually . . . never
   - (B) ever . . . seldom
   - (C) never . . . always
   - (D) ever . . . always

4. _____ a good restaurant near my apartment.
   - (A) There are
   - (B) Is it
   - (C) There is
   - (D) This

5. _____ any mail for me today?
   - (A) Is
   - (B) Are there
   - (C) Are
   - (D) Is there

6. _____ the bookstore open on Saturday?
   - (A) When does
   - (B) What time do
   - (C) Who does
   - (D) What does

7. Forrest Bowlins is a banker. He _____ people's money.
   - (A) manages
   - (B) manage
   - (C) have to
   - (D) wants a

8. Sheldon _____ a nap after school.
   - (A) take
   - (B) does
   - (C) wanting
   - (D) takes

9. Once a week, _____ Fridays, Diane goes dancing.
   - (A) in
   - (B) at
   - (C) on
   - (D) the

10. I celebrate my birthday _____ May 19th.
    - (A) on the
    - (B) in
    - (C) the
    - (D) on

11. A healthy person _____ eat hamburgers every day.
    (A) don't   (B) doesn't
    (C) no   (D) any

12. Chieko _____ want to miss class.
    (A) no   (B) not
    (C) don't   (D) doesn't

13. Enriqueta and Jo _____ about their friend.
    (A) worried   (B) are worry
    (C) are worried   (D) worrying

14. Charlie is always tired. He _____ sleep very well at night.
    (A) no   (B) isn't
    (C) not   (D) doesn't

15. _____ do you get to school? _____.
    (A) How...I take by bus   (B) What...By bus
    (C) How...I take the bus   (D) What...I ride

Identify the one underlined word or phrase that must be changed in order for the sentence to be grammatically correct.

16. She <u>makes plans</u> for her vacation <u>in December</u>. She decides <u>to go skiing</u>, even though
         A   **B**   **C**
    she likes <u>to go the beach</u>.
              D

17. <u>There</u> <u>aren't</u> <u>any</u> milk <u>in</u> the refrigerator.
       A   **B**   **C**   **D**

18. <u>The Italian restaurant</u> is <u>open</u>, but it <u>no have</u> <u>any</u> linguine today.
          A   **B**   **C**   **D**

19. <u>The sun</u> rises <u>always</u> in the east and <u>sets</u> <u>in the west</u>.
        A   **B**   **C**   **D**

20. Many <u>people in India</u> <u>don't eats</u> meat; they <u>only eat</u> vegetables.
         A   **B**   **C**   **D**

21. <u>In the winter</u>, they <u>go for a ski</u> in the <u>mountains</u> <u>in Colorado</u>.
         A   **B**   **C**   **D**

22. <u>Is there</u> anything for the children <u>to do</u> in the <u>summer</u>? They <u>go to swimming</u>.
       A   **B**   **C**   **D**

23. I need <u>to do a phone call</u> before <u>we make a decision</u> about <u>the new car</u>.
       A   **B**   **C**   **D**

24. Blanca <u>doesn't goes</u> to <u>the university</u> <u>on Fridays</u> <u>in December</u>.
              A   **B**   **C**   **D**

25. There is a word I <u>don't know</u>. <u>What means</u> sibling? <u>It means</u> a brother or a sister.
       A   **B**   **C**   **D**

69

Exercise 1 *(Focus 1)*

Using the pictures as cues, write affirmative, negative, or polite **imperative** sentences.

E X A M P L E :   Affirmative: *Stay away!*
                  Negative: *Don't touch!*

1.   Affirmative: _____

     Polite: _____

2.   Affirmative: _____

     Polite: _____

3.   Affirmative: _____

     Negative: _____

4.   Affirmative: _____

     Polite: _____

5. Affirmative: _____

   Polite: _____

6. Affirmative: _____

   Negative: _____

7. Affirmative: _____

   Polite: _____

8. Affirmative: _____

   Negative: _____

Exercise 2 *(Focus 2)*

Study the following **imperatives**. Write the **function** of each imperative after it.

Use

Giving advice
Giving an order
Giving a warning when there is danger
Making a polite request
Politely offering something
Giving directions

EXAMPLE: Caution: Do not puncture or incinerate container. Do not expose to heat c
store at a temperature above 120° F. Keep out of reach of children. Avoi
freezing.

Giving a warning when there is danger

1. In a large bowl, mix the margarine and the sugar well. Beat in the molasses. Add the flour, soda, cloves, cinnamon, ginger, and salt.

   _____

2. Danger: Harmful or Fatal if Swallowed. Read caution on back label carefully.

   _____

3. Bring me that report, Private.

   _____

4. Please, eat some more pot roast, Tom.

   _____

5. Please gift wrap this.

   _____

6. Remember to call us if you have a problem. Eat well and get enough sleep.

   _____

Exercise 3 *(Focus 3)*

Check "yes" if the imperative is appropriate in the situation. Check "no" if it is not appropriate. Check "depends" if you think it could be appropriate in certain situations.

Situation	Imperative	Yes	No	Depends
Example: Son to father:	Give me the car keys!		✔	
1. Police officer to teenager:	Don't drive so fast!			
2. Student to teacher:	Tell me the answer.			
3. Patient to doctor:	Please fill out these insurance forms.			
4. Lawyer to client:	Don't say anything to the police.			
5. Employee to boss:	Give me the report!			
6. Dentist to patient:	Brush your teeth three times a day.			
7. Roommate to roommate:	Please answer the phone.			

Exercise 4 *(Focus 3)*

For each inappropriate imperative from Exercise 3, rewrite the imperative in an appropriate form.

E X A M P L E : *Dad, please give me the car keys.*

_____

_____

_____

_____

_____

_____

UNIT

14

Prepositions of Direction

Exercise 1 *(Focus 1)*

If the sentence is correct, write C in front of it. If the sentence is incorrect, write I in front of it and rewrite the sentence making it correct.

E X A M P L E :   *I* Debbie lives off 1638 Perma Drive.

Debbie lives at 1638 Perma Drive.

——   **1.**   She works at 400 State Street.

——   **2.**   Debbie's office is out of the seventh floor.

——   **3.**   Every morning she is late for work, so Debbie runs on her house.

——   **4.**   She drives out of her driveway.

——   **5.**   She turns left out of her neighborhood and gets on the freeway.

——   **6.**   Debbie gets at the freeway when she gets downtown.

——   **7.**   She jumps out of her car.

——   **8.**   She runs at the elevator.

——   **9.**   She gets off on the seventh floor just in time.

——   **10.**   When her boss arrives, Debbie is off her desk.

Exercise 2 *(Focus 2)*

You need three people for this activity. The first person whispers the directions below to the second person. The second person must follow the directions. The third person writes down what she or he sees the second person do. You should begin outside of your classroom.

E X A M P L E :

Whisper: *Walk into the class.*   Write: *Joseph walks into the classroom.*

1. Walk into the classroom.   _____
2. Run to the desk.   ·   _____
3. Put your book on the desk.   _____
4. Tiptoe away from the desk.   _____
5. Walk back to the desk.   _____
6. Take your book off of the desk. _____
7. Jump out of the classroom.   _____

Change roles. The first person can change the order of the activities.

Exercise 3 *(Focus 2)*

Make up your own exercise like Exercise 2. Make a list of six activities using the prepositions in Focus 2 in your text. Tell your partner to do the activities.

Exercise 4 *(Focus 3)*

Match each sentence with the activity in the picture. The first one has been done for you as an example.

1. The boy walks through the mud.
2. The girl slides down the slide.
3. The joggers run along the path.
4. The girl walks around the mud.
5. The children walk across the balance beam.
6. The children climb up the ladder.
7. The woman runs past the man.
8. The old man walks over the bridge.
9. The boy crawls through the tunnel.
10. The girl swings across the bars.
11. The boy climbs up the bars.

Exercise 5 *(Focus 4)*

Imagine that there is a new student in your class. The student asks you for directions from your classroom to the places below. Write the directions.

EXAMPLE: library: *The library is on the second floor of building 1. Walk downstairs to the first floor. Go across the plaza to building 1. Go up the escalator to the second floor. Turn right and walk to the end of the hall. The library is the last door on the right.*

1. library: _____

_____

_____

_____

_____

_____

2. water fountain: _____

_____

_____

_____

3. registration office: _____

_____

_____

_____

_____

_____

4. cafeteria: _____

_____

_____

_____

_____

_____

5. rest rooms: _____

_____

_____

_____

Exercise 6 *(Focus 4)*

Draw a map showing the way from home to school. Then give directions to your partner. Your partner should follow your directions on the map you drew.

UNIT

15

Direct Objects and
Object Pronouns

Exercise 1 *(Focus 1)*

Look at the picture of Rick. Fill in the blanks with a direct object from the following list.

ball	Rick	soccer
shirt	shoes	game
goal	shorts	stadium
fans	player	points

E X A M P L E :   Rick plays *soccer*.

1. Rick wears a _____ and _____.
2. He hears the _____.
3. The crowd sees _____.
4. Rick loves _____.
5. He kicks the _____.
6. Rick scores a _____.
7. Excitement fills the _____.
8. His team scores the winning _____.
9. He scores more _____ than any other player.
10. Rick's team wins the _____.

78

Exercise 2 *(Focus 2)*

Choose the correct **pronoun** to complete the story. The first one has been done for you as an example.

My dad wakes up in a bad mood. *He* (He, Him) gets a cut while (1) _____ (he, him) is shaving. (2) _____ (He, Him) is grumpy. When my mom gives (3) _____ (he, him) break-fast, (4) _____ (he, him) gets mad at (5) _____ (she, her). This makes my mom angry. (6) _____ (She, Her) yells at my big brother. (7) _____ (She, Her) gets mad at (8) _____ (he, him). My brother shouts at (9) _____ (I, me). (10) _____ (I, me) feel bad. (11) _____ (I, me) yell at Ruff, my dog. Ruff just looks at (12) _____ (I, me). Ruff barks at (13) _____ (I, me) and gives (14) _____ (I, me) a big kiss. The kiss tickles (15) _____ (I, me).

Exercise 3 *(Focus 3)*

Look at the underlined **object pronouns.** Draw an arrow from each object pronoun to the noun phrase it refers to and circle the noun phrase. The first one has been done for you as an example.

I don't feel mad at (my family) any more. I want them to feel happy. I have to do something for them. I go outside and pick some beautiful flowers. I give them to my brother, mother, and father. My brother smiles at me. My mother gives me a kiss. I give her a hug. My father smiles at me too. I give him a hug also. My family is laughing. I really like them when they are happy. Ruff is happy too; my brother is petting him. He finds some milk on the floor and licks it up. When you are happy, everyone is happy with you.

Choose the <u>one</u> word or phrase that best completes the sentence.

1. Kim likes ice cream, but _____ makes her cold.
   (A) she   (B) it
   (C) he   (D) you

2. Artie and Gilberto go _____ Los Angeles every year.
   (A) in   (B) on
   (C) to   (D) at

3. Monica flies _____ San Antonio every week.
   (A) out of   (B) out on
   (C) out off   (D) out at

4. Please, _____ find my keys.
   (A) me help   (B) you help me
   (C) help me   (D) help you

5. The teacher walked _____ the classroom.
   (A) on   (B) through
   (C) off   (D) over

6. Drink water instead of cola. It is more healthy for _____.
   (A) me   (B) him
   (C) you   (D) them

7. Betty has a problem with her daughter. She is always thinking about _____.
   (A) him   (B) she
   (C) them   (D) her

8. Ricardo plays the guitar and practices _____ every day.
   (A) it   (B) onto it
   (C) on them   (D) to it

9. _____! That car is out of control!
   (A) Watch out   (B) Please, turn right
   (C) Put on your blinker   (D) Please, try my new car
       when you turn

10. The marathon race goes _____ the center of the city and _____ the bridge
    (A) through...up   (B) past...through
    (C) through...across   (D) over...down

11. The rice is always overcooked. Please, _____ more carefully.
   - (A) watch it
   - (B) watch them
   - (C) you watch them
   - (D) watch you it

12. A hurricane can blow a roof _____ a house.
   - (A) out of
   - (B) off of
   - (C) at
   - (D) down

13. _____ First Street.
   - (A) Turn left on
   - (B) You turn
   - (C) Turn left into
   - (D) Turn you on

14. There are many fast-food restaurants _____ the highway.
   - (A) to
   - (B) along
   - (C) into
   - (D) out of

15. When the cat and the dog need food I give _____ some.
   - (A) it
   - (B) they
   - (C) them
   - (D) him

Identify the one underlined word or phrase that must be changed in order for the sentence to be grammatically correct.

16. Enrique has many new books; he can read it during the winter break.
   A   B   C   D

17. How often do you call your parents? I call him all the time.
   A   B   C   D

18. Excuse me, how do I get to the park? Go straight. Walk one block. Then
   A   B   C
   turn in the corner of Central Ave.
   D

19. Please, has some more juice. Thanks, it's delicious. Where did you buy it?
   A   B   C
   At the fruit stand.
   D

20. How do I get there? Walk at the corner and turn left.
   A   B   C   D

21. Who likes action movies? Mona likes they; she watches them often.
   A   B   C   D

22. After they climb up the mountain, the explorers climb off of the mountain.
   A   B   C   D

23. This is my best advice about learning a new language. Don't afraid to use it even if you
   A   B   C   D
   make a mistake.

24. The helicopter always flies up the city. The pilot looks for traffic accidents. He tells the
   A   B
   drivers on the ground how to get away from traffic jams.
   C   D

25. The dog likes to play with the cat, but when the dog comes into the house the cat
   A   B
   runs away it.
   C   D

Can versus *Know How To,* And/But

Mrs. and Mr. Sierra have just bought an apartment building. They want to rent it, but the building needs some repairs first. With the help of their daughter, Sisi, they can do many of the repairs. However, they must also hire a plumber, carpenter, and electrician to help them. Here is a list of the things they can do and the things they need help with. Write three sentences about each person. One sentence about what she or he can't do and two sentences about what she or he can do. The first one has been done for you as an example.

Mr. Sierra	**Mrs. Sierra**
Scrape the old paint	Paint the walls
Repair the window screens	Wallpaper the hallway
Plumber	**Carpenter**
Fix the shower	Build kitchen cabinets
Install a hot water heater	Repair the cracked plaster
Electrician	**Sisi**
Install a ceiling fan	Mow the grass
Repair light switches	Rake the leaves

Mr. Sierra

1. *Mr. Sierra can't fix the shower.*
2. _____
3. _____

Mrs. Sierra

1. _____
2. _____
3. _____

The Carpenter

1. _____
2. _____
3. _____

Sisi

1. _____
2. _____
3. _____

Exercise 2 *(Focus 2)* PAIR

Look at the things on the list from Exercise 1. Take turns asking your partner if he or she can do the things on the list.

E X A M P L E : **A:** *Can you fix a shower?*

            B: *No, I can't.* or *Yes, I can.*

Exercise 3 (Focus 2)

Take a survey. Ask three people if they can do the activities on the chart below and fill in their names and responses.

	Name: _____	Name: _____	Name: _____
Speak Cantonese			
Swim			
Drive a car			
Fix a flat tire			
Play a musical instrument			
Cook			

Exercise 4 (Focus 3)

Read the following list. Check each activity which is a learned ability.

Laughing   Reading
Speaking English   Seeing
Riding a bike   Crying
Hearing   Tasting
Flying an airplane   Swimming
Smelling   Writing

Exercise 5 (Focus 3)

Answer the following questions.

What is something you know how to do?

_____

What is something you don't know how to do?

_____

What is something you can do?

_____

What is something you cannot do?

_____

Exercise 6 (Focus 4)

This is a list of things Ali can and can't do. Write sentences about Ali using *and* or *but* as connectors. The first one has been done for you as an example.

Can	**Can't**
swim	dive
float	
paint	make jewelry
draw	
ice skate	ski
ride a sled	
drive a car	repair the engine
fix a flat tire	
wash clothes	sew
iron	

1. *Ali can swim, but he can't dive.*
2. _____
3. _____
4. _____
5. _____
6. _____
7. _____
8. _____
9. _____
10. _____

Exercise 7 (Focus 5)   PAIR

Take turns asking your partner if each of the following statements is correct in English.

1. My mother can cooks the best chicken and rice.
2. I know how to breathe.
3. You can speak English very well.
4. You can fishing from this bridge?
5. Do you know how to play a card game?
6. I can no finish in time.

Adverbs of Manne

PA

Exercise 1 *(Focus 1)*

Ask your partner the following questions. Answer using complete sentences. Write you partner's answer.

E X A M P L E : Are you calm or nervous when you take tests?
I'm calm when I take a test.

1. Are you calm or nervous when you take tests?

   _____

2. Are you grumpy or cheerful when you wake up in the morning?

   _____

3. Are your clothes loose or tight?

   _____

4. Are you a heavy or moderate exerciser?

   _____

5. Are you shy or outgoing when you meet a new person?

   _____

6. Are you slow or quick when you walk somewhere?

   _____

7. Are you careful or careless when you drive?

   _____

Exercise 2 *(Focus 1)*

Write answers to the following questions about your partner based on his or her responses Exercise 1. Use complete sentences.

E X A M P L E : Does your partner take tests calmly?
Yes, she takes tests calmly.

1. Does your partner take tests calmly?

   _____

2. Does your partner wake up grumpily or cheerfully?

   _____

3. Do your partner's clothes fit tightly or loosely?

   _____

4. Does you partner exercise moderately or heavily?

   _____

5. Does your partner meet new people shyly?

   _____

6. Does your partner walk slowly or quickly?

   _____

7. Does you partner drive carefully or carelessly?

   _____

Exercise 3 *(Focus 2)*

Using the information from this story, fill in the blanks in the second story using **adverbs** instead of **adjectives.** The first one has been done for you as an example.

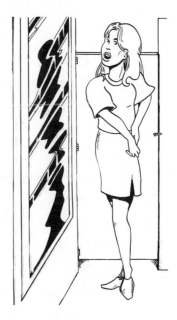

Mom was early coming home, because her shopping trip was terrible. She was enthusiastic when she left the house because there were many new clothes she wanted to buy.

First, she tried on a blue skirt. The skirt looked good, but the fit wasn't terrific. It was loose. So, she tried on a black skirt, but it was tight. When she took the skirt off she was careless, and the zipper broke. She tried to be careful when she fixed the zipper, but it got stuck. She couldn't get the skirt on or off. She became anxious and pulled on the zipper, but it still wouldn't move. She didn't know what to do. Even though she felt shy, she called for a saleswoman. The saleswoman was glad to help. She tried to unzip the skirt, but she was also unsuccessful. Mom was brave. She was calm as she waited. The saleswoman got some scissors and made a neat cut near the zipper. Mom was quick to leave the store.

Mom came home *early*, because her shopping trip went _____. She left _____ because there were many new clothes she wanted to buy.

First she tried on a blue skirt. The skirt looked like it would fit _____, but it didn't fit _____. It fit _____. So she tried on a black skirt but it fit _____. She took the skirt off _____ and the zipper broke. She tried to fix the zipper _____ , but it got stuck. She couldn't get the skirt on or off. She pulled _____ on the zipper, but it still wouldn't move. She didn't know what to do. She called for a saleswoman _____. The saleswoman _____ helped She _____ tried to unzip the skirt. Mom stood _____ and waited _____. The saleswoman got some scissors and cut _____ near the zipper. Mom left the store _____.

Exercise 4 *(Focus 3)*

Think about the different jobs below. Using the cues, write two sentences for each job. On sentence should focus on the **performer;** the other sentence on the **activity.**

E X A M P L E : Receptionist/polite

performer: *A receptionist is polite on the phone.*
activity: *A receptionist answers the phone politely.*

1. Model/attractive

   performer: _____

   activity: _____

2. Waitress/quick

   performer: _____

   activity: _____

3. Nurse/calm

   performer: _____

   activity: _____

4. Truck driver/careful

   performer: _____

   activity: _____

5. Mechanic/messy

   performer: _____

   activity: _____

6. Race car driver/fast

   performer: _____

   activity: _____

7. Scientist/systematic

   performer: _____

   activity: _____

8. Pilot/cautious

   performer: _____

   activity: _____

9. Construction worker/noisy

   performer: _____

   activity: _____

Exercise 5 *(Focus 4)*

Think of a person, place, thing, or activity that fits each category below. Write a sentence using the **intensifier** *very*.

E X A M P L E :   a car that goes fast

A Corvette goes very fast.

1. a basketball player who jumps high

   _____

2. an athlete who runs well

   _____

3. someone in your class who reads quickly

   _____

4. a person who works lazily

   _____

5. someone who sings beautifully

   _____

6. a plant that grows slowly

   _____

7. someone in your class who shops carefully

_____

8. a sexy actress or actor

_____

9. a restaurant where you can buy good food cheaply

_____

10. a writer who writes poetically

_____

11. an animal that runs quickly

_____

Exercise 6 *(Focus 4)*

Compare your answers in Exercise 5 with other group members. Choose your favorite answe for each category. Share those answers with the rest of the students in your class.

Present Progressive Tense

Exercise 1 *(Focus 1)*

I am Jose Villanuevo. This is my family. I have three sisters. Jennifer is my older sister. My two younger sisters Carmen and Margarita are twins. I also have a younger brother Tito and a baby brother, Ricky. We are on vacation. Right now we are having fun at the Wild Water amusement park.

Complete the sentences with the correct form of the **present progressive tense**.

EXAMPLE: Jennifer *is looking* (look) at the lifeguard.

1. Tito _____ (eat) a hot dog.
2. The lifeguard _____ (watch) the swimmers and blowing his whistle.
3. Carmen and Margarita _____ (bury) Dad in the sand.
4. The man _____ (jump) into the water.
5. Mom _____ (buy) the hot dogs and hamburgers.
6. Dad _____ (sleep) on the sand.
7. Ricky _____ (wade).
8. I _____ (slide) down the water slide.
9. The hot dogs _____ (burn).
10. The drinks _____ (spill).

Exercise 2 *(Focus 1)*

Work with a partner. Take turns pointing to an activity in the picture in Exercise 1 and telling each other what's happening.

Exercise 3 *(Focus 2)*

Write a sentence describing each activity using the words in parentheses as cues. Be sure t spell the verb correctly and use the correct form.

E X A M P L E : (Ricky/wade)

Ricky is wading.

1. (Dad/get/sunburn)

   _____

2. (Carmen/dig)

   _____

3. (swimmers/splash)

   _____

4. (the girls/bury/Dad)

   _____

5. (hot dogs/burn)

   _____

6. (I/slide)

   _____

7. (lifeguard/blow/whistle)

   _____

8. (Dad/lie in sand)

   _____

9. (Mom/buy/food)

   _____

10. (Jennifer/flirt)

    _____

11. (Tito/eat)

    _____

Exercise 4 *(Focus 3)*

Now we're on our way home from the water park. Everyone is hot and tired. We aren't having fun now.

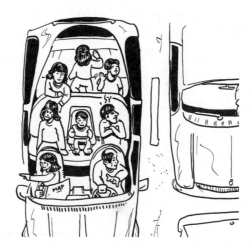

Using the **negative** form, complete sentences describing the picture.

E X A M P L E :   Tito/feel well

Tito isn't feeling well.

1. The family/have fun

    _____

2. Dad/drive carefully

    _____

3. Carmen and Margarita/sit still

    _____

4. Mom/agree with dad

    _____

5. The air conditioning/work

    _____

6. I/talk to my family

    _____

7. Traffic/move

    _____

8. Jennifer/smile

    _____

9. Ricky/sleep

    _____

10. Dad/watch the road

    _____

Exercise 5 *(Focus 3)*

Write the sentences you wrote in Exercise 4 using *negative contractions*.

_____

_____

_____

_____

_____

_____

_____

_____

_____

_____

Exercise 6 *(Focus 4)*

Hello, it's me again! Now everybody in my family is getting ready for Christmas.

Look at the picture. Use the verbs given to write affirmative or negative statements. The fir
one has been done for you.

EXAMPLE: Tito/eat cookies.

Tito is eating cookies.

1. Jennifer/wrap packages

    _____

2. Tito/help mom

    _____

3. Mom/bake cookies

    _____

4. Ricky/sleep

    _____

5. Dad/put up lights

    _____

6. Carmen and Margarita/sing Christmas carols.

    _____

7. I/shovel snow

    _____

8. Cookies/burn

    _____

9. Carmen and Margarita/decorate the Christmas tree

    _____

10. Jennifer/talk on the phone.

    _____

Exercise 7 *(Focus 4)*

Go to a busy place like a mall or a supermarket and write down 10 things you see people doing.

_____

_____

_____

_____

_____

_____

_____

_____

_____

_____

Exercise 8 *(Focus 5)*

Read the story. If the underlined verb describes an action in progress write a *P* on the line i
front of the sentence. If the underlined verb describes a **temporary action** or a **changin**
situation write *T/C* in front of the sentence.

E X A M P L E :   *T/C* Dad is under a lot of stress. But, this year he's <u>taking</u> better care
himself.

1. _____ These days, he <u>is jogging</u> more often.
2. _____ He <u>is jogging</u> right now.
3. _____ He <u>is also trying</u> to eat better.
4. _____ Nowadays, he <u>is eating</u> more fruits and vegetables and less junk food.
5. _____ These days he <u>is also spending</u> more time with his family.
6. _____ But that <u>isn't helping</u> his stress.
7. _____ The kids <u>are jogging</u> with him.
8. _____ They <u>are driving</u> him crazy.

Exercise 9 *(Focus 5)*   INDIVIDUAL, GROL

Complete each of the following sentences to tell about an action that is temporary or
situation that is changing in your life. Then choose some of the sentences you wrote ar
share them with your classmates.

1. This week... _____
2. Today... _____
3. These days... _____
4. This month... _____
5. Nowadays... _____
6. This year..... _____

Exercise 10 *(Focus 6)*

At Christmas time things are different around my house. We aren't doing the things that we
usually do.

Complete each complex sentence below by adding a phrase in the **simple present** or t
present progressive. Use *but* to connect the two phrases. Be sure to use the correct tin
expression in your answer.

EXAMPLE: I usually go to school, *but today I'm shoveling snow*.

1. I'm usually in math class right now, _____.

2. _____ today he's putting up the Christmas lights.

3. Mom rarely makes cookies, _____.

4. _____ now she isn't at her boyfriend's house.

5. Ricky usually takes a nap, _____.

6. _____ at the moment he's eating cookies.

7. _____ at present they are arguing over a decoration.

8. Mom usually takes care of Ricky during the day, _____.

9. Dad usually helps me shovel the snow, _____.

10. Tito usually eats good food, _____.

Exercise 11 *(Focus 7)*

Read the following sentences. Put both of the verbs at the end of the sentence in their correct place in the sentence. Be sure to use the correct form of each verb.

EXAMPLE: Dad *seems* impatient; he *is honking* the horn. (honk, seem)

1. He _____ the bun, so he _____ the meat. (not eat, prefer)

2. That radio _____ wet; it _____ to me. (get, belong)

3. Mom always _____ where she put her keys; she _____ for them. (look, forget)

4. I _____ something funny; the hot dogs _____. (burn, smell)

5. I _____ a good job, but I _____ problems with my boss. (have, have)

6. Tito _____ again; that boy _____ food. (love, eat)

7. The water park _____ nice; the kids _____ fun. (seem, have)

8. The car _____ to dad, but he _____ trouble with the air conditioning. (have, belong)

9. They _____ in God; that's why they _____ to church. (go, believe)

Exercise 12 *(Focus 8)*

Choose an appropriate verb. Then make questions. Ask your partner the questions. Record his or her short answers.

EXAMPLE: You/ .../ other classes

Are you taking other classes?

Yes, I am.

study	pass	get	live	improve	speak
help	take	practice	ask	have	

1. You / ... / this class _____
2. Your English / ... _____
3. You / ... / your classmates _____
4. You / ... / English at home _____
5. You / ... / English grammar _____
6. English grammar / ... / easier _____
7. You / ... / good day _____
8. I / ... / questions correctly _____
9. Your mother / ... / in the United States _____
10. I / ... / clearly _____

Exercise 13 *(Focus 9)*

Now we are getting ready for a big family reunion. There are so many people that Mom made a list of who is coming, what food they are bringing, when they are coming, how they are coming, and where they are sleeping. I hope they bring enough food for Tito!

Look at the lists, and write 15 questions about the people coming to the family reunion. Use as many different question words as possible. Then answer the questions you write. There are many correct answers to this exercise. Compare your answers to your classmates'.

EXAMPLE: When are Grandma and Grandpa arriving?

They are arriving Friday morning.

Who	What	When	How	Where
Grandma & Grandpa	Potato Salad	Friday Morning	Car	Twins' room
Uncle Manuel	Drinks	Friday 7:00 A.M.	Train	Living room
Cousin Carla & her husband	Fresh Fruit	Friday Noon	Plane	Jose's room
Aunt Luz	Cake	Friday Evening	Car	Guest room
Uncle Raul	Chips	Friday Morning	Bus	Garage

1. _____
   _____

2. _____
   _____

3. _____
   _____

4. _____
   _____

5. _____
   _____

6. _____
   _____

7. _____
   _____

8. _____
   _____

9. _____
   _____

10. _____
    _____

11. _____
    _____

12. _____
    _____

13. _____
    _____

14. _____
    _____

15. _____
    _____

Choose the <u>one</u> word or phrase that best completes the sentence.

1. _____ a musical instrument?
   - (A) Can you playing
   - (B) Can you play
   - (C) You can to play
   - (D) You play

2. I can sing, but I _____ play a musical instrument.
   - (A) canot
   - (B) no can
   - (C) can't
   - (D) can

3. Many of my friends play music _____.
   - (A) beauty
   - (B) beautifully
   - (C) beautifuly
   - (D) beautiful

4. Do they _____ play the guitar?
   - (A) can
   - (B) cannot
   - (C) know how to
   - (D) can't

5. My friend, Simon, plays _____.
   - (A) professional guitar
   - (B) professionally guitar
   - (C) guitar professional
   - (D) guitar professionally

6. He _____ every day. In fact, he _____ right now.
   - (A) is practicing . . . practices
   - (B) practices . . . is practicing
   - (C) practice . . . is practicing
   - (D) practices . . . practicing

7. Where _____?
   - (A) does he practicing
   - (B) he practices
   - (C) does he
   - (D) is he practicing

8. He _____ practices at his mother's house.
   - (A) right now
   - (B) at this moment
   - (C) nowadays
   - (D) usually

9. _____ he plays in an elegant bar.
   - (A) Now
   - (B) Tonight
   - (C) At this moment
   - (D) Every weekend

10. Simon _____ to play Spanish guitar music.
    - (A) is preferring
    - (B) prefer
    - (C) prefers
    - (D) is prefers

11. Now he _____ on some new songs.
    (A) is working   (B) will work
    (C) works   (D) working

12. Right now he is playing guitar at the bar on the weekends, but he _____ guitar at the bar during the week.
    (A) 's not playing   (B) is playing
    (C) are not playing   (D) plays

13. _____ his job? Yes, he _____ .
    (A) Does he enjoy . . . is   (B) Is he enjoying . . . is
    (C) Are we enjoying . . . are   (D) Is he enjoy . . . is

14. His boss pays him _____ , but he must work _____ .
    (A) very good . . . lately   (B) well very . . . late
    (C) very good . . . late   (D) very well . . . late

15. That's great. He can enjoy his work _____ a lot of money.
    (A) and make   (B) but can make
    (C) but can't make   (D) and cannot make

Identify the one underlined word or phrase that must be changed in order for the sentence to be grammatically correct.

16. We're going to the beach. Can Ellen come? Does she can swim?
    A   B   C   D

17. Ellen is afraid of water, but this week she are bravely learning how to swim.
                       A   B   C   D

18. Where is she taking lessons? At the pool; she is going there every day.
    A   B   C   D

19. Every morning, she walks to the pool. She timidly puts her toe in the water.
               A   B   C   D

20. At first, she is hating the water, but once she jumps in, she splashes happily.
             A   B   C   D

21. She can no swim perfectly, but she is learning quickly.
       A   B   C   D

22. She knows how to breathe. Now she is learning how to breathe when she is swimming.
     A   B   C   D

23. She can goes to the beach, but please watch her carefully.
    A B   C   D

24. She cannot swim good. She needs someone near her when she is swimming.
     A   B   C   D

25. We always stay in shallow water and we always are watching little children very carefully.
         A   B   C   D

26. Can your brother makes model airplanes? Yes, this week he is building a new model.
    A   B   C   D

27. He can put the pieces together, and he can't paint the model by himself. He needs help.
    A B   C   D

28. Who helping him with this model? My mother is helping him. She can paint the small
        $\overline{\text{A}}$ $\overline{\text{B}}$ $\overline{\text{C}}$ $\overline{\text{D}}$
    details.

29. First, before he builds a model, he reads all the directions one time fastly. That way he
                    $\overline{\text{A}}$ $\overline{\text{B}}$
    can make sure he has everything he needs.
        $\overline{\text{C}}$ $\overline{\text{D}}$

30. When he starts the model, he very reads carefully. He makes sure he follows the direc-
                $\overline{\text{A}}$ $\overline{\text{B}}$ $\overline{\text{C}}$
    tions correctly.
            $\overline{\text{D}}$

UNIT

19

Past Tense of *Be*

Exercise 1 *(Focus 1)*

This story is a story similar to the story of Cinderella, but it is from Canadian Indians who live on the Atlantic coast of North America.

Complete the story using *was* or *were*. The first one has been done for you as an example.

The Indian Cinderella

Once there *was* an Indian maiden. Her mother _____ dead, so her sisters took care of her. The maiden _____ very beautiful, and her sisters _____ jealous. They _____ mean to her. They made her do all the work. The older sisters _____ rich, but the maiden's clothes _____ old rags.

In the same village, there _____ a great warrior named Strong Wind, the Invisible. He _____ very powerful. He _____ different from all the other warriors because he could make himself invisible. Many girls in the village wanted to be Strong Wind's wife. When Strong Wind _____ ready to marry, he made an announcement. He would marry whoever could see him when he was invisible.

The three sisters all wanted to marry Strong Wind.

The first sister said, "I see Strong Wind. He is there," but she was lying. She couldn't see him at all.

The second sister said, "Yes, I see him, he's there." But she _____ not truthful either.

The Indian maiden looked and looked, then said, "No, I cannot see him." She _____ honest.

Strong Wind liked her honesty, so he made himself visible only to her. Then the maiden shouted "I see Strong Wind." Strong Wind became visible to all the people of the village and they saw she was telling the truth.

The two sisters _____ angry and tried to hurt the maiden. But Strong Wind turned them into aspen trees. That is why the aspen trees shake when Strong Wind passes. Strong Wind and the maiden _____ married and they _____ very happy together.

Exercise 2 *(Focus 2)*

Using the list of characters and descriptions, write five **negative statements** about the characters in "The Indian Cinderella." Then make a true **affirmative statement.** There are many correct answers to this exercise. Compare your answers with your classmates.

E X A M P L E : *Strong Wind was not weak. He was powerful.*

Characters	Descriptions	
Strong Wind	honest	a great warrior
Sisters	beautiful	nice
Maiden	powerful	jealous
	weak	happy
	angry	dishonest
	rich	poor

1. _____

2. _____

3. _____

4. _____

5. _____

Exercise 3 (Focus 2)

Make the following statements true by changing them into **negative statements.**

E X A M P L E : There was a mother in the story.
There was not a mother in the story.

1. The story was about two good sisters.

    _____

2. The maiden's clothes were new.

    _____

3. There was a princess in the story.

    _____

4. The maiden was unhappy at the end of the story.

    _____

5. The story was sad at the end.

    _____

Exercise 4 (Focus 2)

PAIR, GROUP

Tell a partner three things about how you felt when you first arrived in the United States. Then tell the rest of your classmates how your partner felt. Use the word list to help you.

E X A M P L E : You tell your partner: *I was afraid when I first arrived in the United States.*
Your partner tells the class: *She was afraid.*

upset	excited	tired	interested	mad
happy	angry	frightened	sleepy	shy
afraid	sad			

Exercise 5 *(Focus 3)*

Read the answers. Write the *yes/no* questions.

EXAMPLE: *Were the sisters nice to the maiden?*

No, they were not nice to the maiden.

1. _____

   Yes, there were three sisters.

2. _____

   Yes, her sisters were rich.

3. _____

   Yes, the sisters were jealous and mean.

4. _____

   No, her clothes weren't new.

5. _____

   Yes, he was a powerful warrior.

6. _____

   No, they weren't honest.

7. _____

   Yes, she was honest.

8. _____

   No, the sisters were not married.

9. _____

   Yes, the ending was happy.

Exercise 6 *(Focus 3)*

PAIR

Find out about your partner. Ask how he or she was as a child. Check "yes" or "no" depending on the answer.

EXAMPLE: *When you were a child, were you neat?*

Partner's name: _____

	Yes	No		Yes	No
Neat	—	—	Good in school	—	—
Helpful	—	—	Funny	—	—
Happy	—	—	Messy	—	—
Sad	—	—			

Exercise 7 *(Focus 4)*

Create 10 sentences that contrast past and present meaning using *but*. Each sentence should contain one word or phrase from each box. There are many correct answers. Compare your answers with your classmates to see how many different correct answers you can make.

E X A M P L E S :   *Last year English was difficult for me, but this year it is easy.*
English is easy this year, but it was difficult last year.

yesterday	I	today	excited	happy
last night	my parents	this year	clean	unhappy
yesterday morning	my teacher	tonight	neat	sad
last year	my classmates	this morning	broken	angry
before	my car	now	fixed	homesick
	my friend	this time	pretty	beautiful
	my clothes		old	ugly
	my house (apartment)		new	easy
	you		busy	difficult
	we		lazy	soft
	my family		hard	noisy
	English			

1. _____

_____

2. _____

_____

3. _____

_____

4. _____

_____

5. _____

_____

6. _____

_____

7. _____

_____

8. _____

_____

9. _____

_____

10. _____

Exercise 8 *(Focus 5)*

Imagine that you were a newspaper reporter who attended the wedding of Strong Wind and the Indian maiden. You interviewed one of the wedding guests to find out how the bride and groom met. Write the questions you asked. Be sure to use *be* in the simple past.

E X A M P L E : What *was she like before they met?*

1. What _____

2. When _____

3. Where _____

4. Why _____

5. How _____

6. Whose sisters _____

7. Who _____

Exercise 9 *(Focus 5)*

PAI!

Take turns asking and answering your questions from Exercise 8 with a partner.

UNIT

20

Past Tense

Exercise 1 *(Focus 1)*

Complete the story with the **past tense** form of the verb. Check your spelling. The first one has been done for you as an example.

Bernie Bungle *tried* (try) to rob the Midnight Market, but Bernie was not a very good robber. This is what happened to him:

Bernie _____(plan) to rob the store early in the morning, but he overslept, so he _____(arrive) late.

When he got to the store he _____(study) the cashier and customers carefully to make sure there were no police. Then, he _____ (cover) his face with a nylon stocking, but the stocking was too thick, so he couldn't see very well. That is why he _____ (trip) when he _____ (enter) the store. All the customers _____ (turn) and _____ (look) at him.

Bernie _____ (point) his gun at the cashier and _____ (demand) all the money. The cashier _____ (fill) up a paper bag with money and _____ (hand) it to Bernie.

After he _____ (rob) the store, Bernie _____ (try) to escape, but the money bag _____ (rip) and some of the money _____ (drop) out of the bag. When Bernie _____ (hop) into his car, he _____ (remember) why he _____ (want) to rob the store early in the morning. There was a traffic jam and he couldn't go anywhere.

The police _____ (worry) that the robber would get away. But when they _____ (arrive) there was Bernie only one block away.

109

Exercise 2 *(Focus 2)*

Your teacher will read the following words to you in the **past tense**. Listen to the end sound. Write each word in the correct column depending on its end sound.

At School:	At Work:	Cleaning House:	At the Playground:
learn	walk	vacuum	play
study	fix	iron	jump
listen	work	clean	enjoy
remember	file	wash	skate
print	type	brush	hop
discuss	deliver	polish	bounce
answer	lock	changed	trip
name	start	baked	climb
correct	point	dust	skip
ask	talk	scrub	kiss

Group I: /t/	Group II: /d/	Group III: /id/

Exercise 3 *(Focus 2)*

With the other members of your group, make a past tense chain story using a group of verbs from above. To make a chain story, one member of the group starts the story using one of the words from the list. The next person in the group continues the story. Each person in the group adds to the story. Make sure that each member of the group pronounces the **past tense** verb correctly.

Exercise 4 (Focus 3)

Complete the story with the **past tense** form of the verb. The first one has been done for you as an example.

As soon as Bernie Bungle _got_ (get) out of jail, he _____ (get) in trouble again.

Bernie _____ (see) a house. It _____ (look) like no one was home. Bernie _____ (break) the window and _____ (go) in. He _____ (look) for something to steal. Bernie _____ (find) some jewelry and _____ (put) it into a pillow case.

As he _____ (look) around for something else to steal, he _____ (begin) to feel hungry. So he _____ (take) a look in the kitchen. He _____ (find) a frozen pizza and some beer. Bernie _____ (heat) the pizza and _____ (make) himself some lunch. He _____ (eat) the pizza and _____ (drink) all the beer. Then Bernie _____ (feel) a little tired so he _____ (sit) down and _____ (fall) asleep.

As he _____ (sleep), Mr. Chan _____ (come) home. When he _____ (see) Bernie sleeping in the chair, Mr. Chan _____ (call) the police.

Bernie _____ (hear) him and _____ (wake) up. He _____ (stand) up and _____ (run) out of the house. However, the police _____ (catch) Bernie on his way out. He _____ (go) to jail once more.

Exercise 5 (Focus 4)

Today is October 31. David Johnson is the gardener at Pine Cone College. He has a bus schedule. The calendar shows what he did in the last month. Write a sentence about th calendar for each of the **time expressions** below.

Sunday	Monday	Tuesday	Wednesday	Thursday	Friday	Saturday
29	30	1 *rake leaves*	2 *mow grass*	3 *trim hedges*	4 *fertilize trees*	5
6	7 *trim trees*	8 *rake leaves*	9 *mow grass*	10 *repair sprinklers*	11 *spray for insects*	12
13	14 *repair equipment*	15 *rake leaves*	16 *mow grass*	17 *trim hedges*	18	19
20	21	22 *rake leaves*	23 *mow grass*	24 *plant flowers*	25 *repair sprinklers*	26
27	28 *check tools*	29 *rake leaves*	30 *morning trim hedges afternoon mow grass night set-up president's party*	31	1	2

1. (yesterday) _____

2. (last week) _____

3. (two days ago) _____

4. (on Monday) _____

5. (yesterday morning) _____

6. (last night) _____

7. (the day before yesterday) _____

8. (two weeks ago) _____

9. (last Friday) _____

10. (yesterday afternoon) _____

Exercise 6 *(Focus 4)*

Write a sentence telling what you did at each time given.

EXAMPLE: (yesterday afternoon)

Yesterday afternoon, I went out for lunch.

1. (yesterday afternoon) _____

2. (last night) _____

3. (last weekend) _____

4. (six months ago) _____

5. (last year) _____

6. (the day before yesterday) _____

7. (an hour ago) _____

8. (last month) _____

Exercise 7 *(Focus 5)*

Make the following statements true by using the negative form in the past tense.

EXAMPLE: Bernie woke up on time on the day he robbed the Midnight Market.

Bernie didn't wake up on time the day he robbed the Midnight Market.

1. Bernie wore a ski mask on his head. _____

   _____

2. Bernie got away after he robbed the Midnight Market._____

   _____

3. Bernie learned his lesson after robbing the Midnight Market._____

   _____

4. Bernie broke the door when he robbed Mr. Chan's house._____

   _____

5. Bernie bought some jewelry at the store. _____

   _____

6. Bernie stole Mr. Chan's TV. _____

   _____

7. Bernie ate a sandwich. _____

   _____

8. Bernie drank some coffee. _____

_____

9. Bernie slept in a bed. _____

_____

10. Mr. Chan called the fire department. _____

_____

11. Bernie drove away in his car from Mr. Chan's house._____

_____

12. Bernie escaped from the police two times. _____

Exercise 8 *(Focus 6)*

Can you remember what you did when you were in elementary school? Using the cues, tak turns with your partner asking about each other's elementary school experience.

E X A M P L E : *Did you wear a uniform to school?*
        Yes, I did.

Ask your partner if she or he

1. wore a uniform to school	6. sang songs
2. helped the teacher	7. liked her or his teachers
3. studied hard	8. played sports
4. rode a bus to school	9. (her or his parents) bought her or h
5. got good grades	books
	10. said "Good morning" to the teacher

Exercise 9 *(Focus 7)*

Imagine that you are a newspaper reporter. You heard the story about Bernie Bungle th burglar. You want to ask the victims questions about Bernie's two crimes. Use the *wh*-word and cues to write the questions you want to ask. The first one has been done for you as a example.

The Cashier at the Midnight Market

1. why/trip *Why did he trip when he entered the store?* _____

2. Where/put money _____

3. What/happen to the money _____

4. What/police do _____

5. Where/police catch _____

Mr. Chan

6. What/happen _____

7. How/get in _____

8. Who/find _____

9. Where/find him _____

10. What/do _____

11. How long/sleep _____

Indirect Objects with To

Exercise 1 *(Focus 1)*

Kim and Wan-Yin are excited. They are seniors. They are going to graduate from high school next week. They have just been accepted at the University of Hawaii. They want to thank all the people who helped them. They made a list of those people and how they helped them.

Read the lists. Write the **direct object** for each sentence in the first column and the **indirect object** in the second column. The first one has been done for you as an example.

Kim

1. The counselor wrote a letter of recommendation to the University of Hawaii.
2. Kim's mom mailed the graduation announcements to his family.
3. Wan-Yin sent flowers to Kim.
4. Aunt Chin sent books to Kim.
5. Kim's dad gave a calculator to Kim.

Wan-Yin

6. Mr. Dickens, the English teacher, taught composition to Wan-Yin.
7. Wan-Yin's parents paid the college admission fee to the University.
8. Uncle Yee gave a ream of paper to Wan-Yin.
9. Kim gave a pen set to Wan-Yin.
10. Wan-Yin's grandmother sent money to her.

	Direct Object	Indirect Object
1.	*letter*	*University of Hawaii*
2.		
3.		
4.		
5.		
6.		
7.		
8.		
9.		
10.		

Exercise 2 (Focus 2)

Rewrite the sentences in Exercise 1 with the **indirect object** before the **direct object**. The first one has been done for you as an example.

1. _The counselor wrote the University of Hawaii a letter of recommendation._

2. _____

3. _____

4. _____

5. _____

6. _____

7. _____

8. _____

9. _____

10. _____

Exercise 3 (Focus 3)

At Christmas time Practical Pete gives at least a small present to everyone. Here are the things he gave this year. Use the list to answer the questions below.

EXAMPLE: Who(m) did Pete give socks to?

Pete gave socks to Brad.

Christmas gift list
Mom: dish towels
Dad: flashlight
Angela and Bob (Pete's sister and brother-in-law): car wax
Brad (Pete's nephew): socks
Secretary: dictionary
Cecelia (Pete's girlfriend): hair brush
Mail carrier: dog repellant
The neighbors: screwdriver set

1. What did Pete give the neighbors?

   _____

2. Who(m) did Pete give the hair brush to?

   _____

3. What did Pete give the mail carrier?

   _____

4. What did Pete give his girlfriend?

_____

5. Who(m) did Pete give the dictionary to?

_____

6. What did Pete give to his dad?

_____

7. Who(m) did Pete give the dish towels to?

_____

8. Who(m) did Pete give the car wax to?

_____

9. What did Pete give to his secretary?

_____

10. Who(m) did Pete give the screwdriver set to?

_____

Exercise 4 *(Focus 3)*

Pete always gives practical gifts, but they aren't always the best gifts. What gifts do you thin
would be more appropriate? Write four sentences emphasizing **what** they will receive ar
four sentences emphasizing **who** will receive it.

E X A M P L E : *Pete will give his mother some perfume.* (emphasis is on what)

Who

1. _____

2. _____

3. _____

4. _____

What

1. _____

2. _____

3. _____

4. _____

Exercise 5 (Focus 4)

Underline the **indirect object**. Then change the underlined words to **pronouns**.

E X A M P L E : I sent my letter of application to the admissions officers.
I sent them my letter of application.

1. Kim handed Wan-Yin his calculator.

    _____

2. Wan-Yin introduced Kim to her mother and father.

    _____

3. Wan-Yin showed Mr. Dickens her essay.

    _____

4. Kim taught it to Wan-Yin.

    _____

5. Aunt Chin offered Kim help.

    _____

6. Kim sent a thank you note to the counselor and me.

    _____

7. I repeated what Kim's mom said to Kim.

    _____

8. She explained the problem to Kim.

    _____

9. I read my sons the book.

    _____

Exercise 6 (Focus 5)

Read the story. Rewrite the underlined sentences with the **indirect object** before the **direct object** if possible. The first one has been done for you as an example.

Getting accepted at a good university is not easy. Wan-Yin worked hard to get accepted at the University of Hawaii.

First, she had to take the SAT test. The math section was the most difficult for Wan-Yin. Kim helped her with her math. (1) He showed some math shortcuts to Wan-Yin. (2) He explained the math problems to her. (3) He also lent his calculator to her.

After she took the SAT test, Wan-Yin had to fill out an application form. The most difficult part of the application was the essay. Wan-Yin asked her English teacher for help.

(4) She brought the essay to Mr. Dickens. (5) Then she read the essay to him. (6) M Dickens gave suggestions to her on ways to improve the essay. The counselor also helpe her. She wrote a letter of recommendation to the University of Hawaii. (7) Then Wan-Yi mailed the application to the University.

She was excited when she heard she was accepted. However, she had another problem She didn't have enough money to pay for tuition. So she went to the University to see an ad missions officer. (8) She showed her good grades and SAT scores to him. (9) She describe her problem to him. (10) The admissions officer sent Wan-Yin to a financial aid counselo (11) At the financial aid office, the counselor handed the forms to her.

Wan-Yin was lucky she got a scholarship to help pay for her education.

1. *He showed Wan-Yin some math shortcuts.*

2. _____

3. _____

4. _____

5. _____

6. _____

7. _____

8. _____

9. _____

10. _____

11. _____

Choose the <u>one</u> word or phrase that best completes the sentence.

1. _____ do last night?
   - (A) What you did
   - (B) What did you
   - (C) Did you
   - (D) You did

2. Last night, I _____ my mother.
   - (A) visited
   - (B) visit
   - (C) am visiting
   - (D) visits

3. _____ dinner at her house? Yes, I did.
   - (A) What did you eat
   - (B) Did you ate
   - (C) What were you
   - (D) Did you eat

4. Yesterday, my mother _____ spaghetti for dinner. It _____ delicious.
   - (A) maked . . . were
   - (B) makes . . . is
   - (C) made . . . were
   - (D) made . . . was

5. She gave _____ the leftover spaghetti.
   - (A) me
   - (B) to me
   - (C) my
   - (D) to I

6. She also _____ my clothes, but she _____ them for me.
   - (A) washed . . . ironed
   - (B) didn't wash . . . didn't iron
   - (C) washed . . . didn't iron
   - (D) washed . . . didn't ironed

7. _____, I wasn't living in North America.
   - (A) Three months ago
   - (B) Three last months
   - (C) At three months ago
   - (D) In three months ago

8. Last year, I _____ Russia.
   - (A) leave
   - (B) am leaving
   - (C) leaved
   - (D) left

9. The U.S. government _____ me to the United States when an American family _____ to sponsor me last winter.
   - (A) admitted . . . agreeded
   - (B) admit . . . agree
   - (C) admits . . . agrees
   - (D) admitted . . . agreed

10. The Rosenburg family _____.
    - (A) sended to me some money
    - (B) sent me some money
    - (C) sended some money to me
    - (D) sent to me some money

11. They were nice. They _____ me find a new job when I arrived in the United States.

    (A) helped   (B) helpped

    (C) didn't help   (D) help

12. When I first _____ to the United States, I _____ happy.

    (A) came . . . wasn't   (B) did come . . . were not

    (C) came . . . didn't be   (D) come . . . were not

13. In the beginning, I wrote _____ every day.

    (A) letters to me family   (B) to my family letters

    (C) letters to my family   (D) my family to letters

14. I described _____.

    (A) everything to them   (B) them everything

    (C) my family everything   (D) everything them

15. I also _____ one week ago.

    (A) mail pictures to them   (B) mailed them pictures

    (C) mailed to them pictures   (D) mail them pictures

Identify the one underlined word or phrase that must be changed in order for the sentence to be grammatically correct.

16. What did Ms. Welch taught in grammar class yesterday?
     A   B   C   D

17. Yesterday morning the lesson is easy. We reviewed past tense verbs and practiced using
              A   B   C   D
the verbs in sentences.

18. Where were you yesterday? I no see you at school.
     A   B   C D

19. I was absent because I was very sick. I haved a stomach ache.
        A   B   C   D

20. What made you sick? Last night, I eaten something bad and I got food poisoning.
      A   B   C   D

21. I was so sick. It was terrible. Finally, I told my dad that I wasn't feel well.
     A   B   C   D

22. Dad drove to the doctor me. I was glad my dad was home.
       A   B   C   D

23. What did the doctor say? He explained me the problem and gave me some medicine.
     A   B   C   D

24. Did the medicine help? Yes, it didn't. It made me feel better.
     A   B   C   D

25. After the pharmacy delivered the medicine to me, I taked two pills. I felt better after I
                A   B   C   D
slept for a while.

26. The same thing happened to me last year ago, but I had to go to the hospital.
            A   B   C   D

27. That's terrible. You really <u>were</u> sick. <u>How long you stayed</u> in the hospital? <u>I was</u> there
       $\quad\quad\quad\quad\quad\quad\quad\quad$ **A** $\quad\quad\quad\quad\quad\quad$ **B** $\quad\quad\quad\quad$ **C** $\quad\quad\quad\quad\quad\quad\quad\quad\quad$ **D**
   only one day.

28. I really <u>felt</u> awful when <u>I was</u> in the hospital. <u>I worryed</u> about paying <u>the bill</u>.
       $\quad\quad\quad$ **A** $\quad\quad\quad\quad\quad$ **B** $\quad\quad\quad\quad\quad\quad$ **C** $\quad\quad\quad\quad\quad$ **D**

29. I <u>explained</u> my sister the <u>problem</u>. She <u>helped</u> me. <u>She called</u> the rest of my family.
       $\quad$ **A** $\quad\quad\quad\quad\quad$ **B** $\quad\quad\quad\quad$ **C** $\quad\quad$ **D**

30. My family <u>offered</u> to help <u>me</u>. They <u>paid</u> some of the bills. They <u>told to me</u> not to
       $\quad\quad\quad\quad$ **A** $\quad\quad\quad$ **B** $\quad\quad$ **C** $\quad\quad\quad\quad\quad\quad\quad\quad$ **D**
   worry.

UNIT 22

Reflexive and Reciproca[l] Pronoun[s]

Exercise 1 *(Focus 1 and 2)*

Write the correct **reflexive pronoun** in the spaces provided in the dialogue. The first on[e] has been done for you as an example.

Paul and Charlotte are having a Halloween party. For the first time, they are putting on [a] party all by *themselves*. They are a little nervous.

Charlotte: Are you ok? What happened?

Paul: I'm fine. I just cut (1) _____ a little when I was carving the jack-o-lantern.

Charlotte: You should wash that cut and get (2) _____ a bandage.

Paul: OK. Should I put the jack-o-lantern by the ghost decoration?

Charlotte: No, put it over there alone, by (3) _____. It will look more scary. Hov[w] do you like my spider web decorations? I made them all by (4) _____[.]

Paul: Great! They look frightening. This is going to be a fun party. I hope the guests enjo[y] (5) _____.

Charlotte: I'm sure everyone will have fun. By the way, who's Brad bringing?

Paul: He couldn't find a date. I guess he's coming by (6) _____.

Charlotte: Well, make sure you pay attention to the other guests too. Sometimes you an[d] Brad go off by (7) _____.

Paul: Don't worry. I'll spend time with the guests.

Charlotte: Do you think I should pour the drinks now or let the guests help (8) _____

Paul: Just let them help (9) _____. I hope the guests arrive soon. I don't want us t[o] have to eat all this food by (10) _____.

Charlotte: They will be here soon. Oh, we aren't in our costumes yet. We have to get (11) _____ ready. Will you help me with my costume? I can't zip it u[p] by (12) _____.

124

Exercise 2 *(Focus 2)*

Decide if the following spaces require a **reflexive pronoun**. If they do, write the correct pronoun in the space. If they do not, put an *X* in the space. The first one has been done for you as an example.

The story continues:

Charlotte: I'm all dirty from making those spider webs. First I think I'll shower <u>X</u> and after I dry _____ you can help me with the zipper.

Paul: OK. While you're doing that I'll shave _____ and then dress _____.

Charlotte: What if the guests arrive early?

Paul: We can blame _____ if they arrive early. I'm sure they can introduce _____. It won't take us long to dress _____.

Paul: See, I told you the guests would enjoy _____. Everyone is dancing and laughing. It looks like Brad has even found _____ a date. I knew he wouldn't have to be all by _____.

Charlotte: You're right, they are all amusing _____. This is a great costume party. Look at Cindy's costume.

Paul: What is she? She looks like she killed _____.

Charlotte: She's the bride of Frankenstein.

Exercise 3 *(Focus 2)*   PAIR

Tell your partner something

1. you can do by yourself.
2. you want to do by yourself.
3. your family did without any help.

Tell someone else what your partner can do.

E X A M P L E : You say: *I can fix my car by myself.*
Your partner says: *She can fix her car by herself.*

Exercise 4 (Focus 3)

Match each picture with the sentence that describes it. The first one has been done for you as an example.

1. The children are spraying themselves with water.
2. The children are spraying each other with water.
3. They are spinning themselves around.
4. They are spinning each other around.
5. They're hot. They are fanning themselves.
6. They're hot. They are fanning each other.
7. They are putting makeup on themselves.
8. They are putting makeup on each other.
9. They are washing their faces.
10. They are washing each other.

<u>1</u>

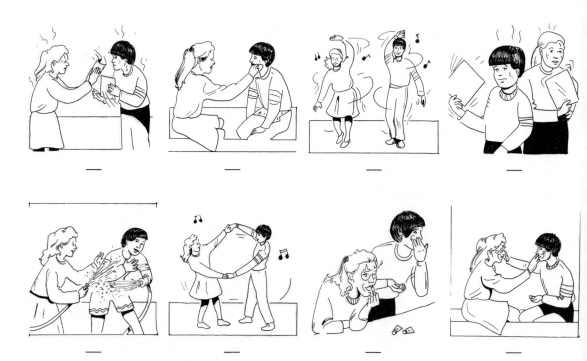

126

Future Time

Exercise 1 *(Focus 1)*

Clumsy Clair reads her horoscope every day. For the past week her horoscope has come true. Match each picture with the day the prediction appeared in her horoscope. Then match what Clair thought when her horoscope came true. Write it under the picture. The first one has been done for you as an example.

Tuesday: I'm going to need a new watch.

_____

_____

_____

_____

_____

_____

_____

_____   _____
_____   _____
_____   _____

Horoscopes

Sunday: You'll get to see nature up close.
Monday: You will buy a new car.
Tuesday: Time will stand still for you.
Wednesday: This will be your lucky day!
Thursday: You will go on a trip.
Friday: A stranger will sweep you off your feet.
Saturday: You'll meet a new love interest.

_____
_____
_____

What Clair thought

My knee is going to hurt!
I'm going to need a new watch.
He's going to think I'm clumsy.
My car insurance is going to increase.
I'm going to call the exterminator.
Now, I'm going to break my arm.
I'm going to put my lottery ticket in a safe place.

Exercise 2 *(Focus 1)*

Find the horoscope section in a newspaper or magazine. Circle the words in the horoscopes which predict future events. Share the horoscopes with your classmates.

Exercise 3 *(Focus 2)*

Here are some yearbook picture of seniors at Hilly High School. Read the yearbook captions. Then write a prediction of what each person will do in the future. The first on has been done for you as an example.

Alice Cooper
Dream: To sing
in a rock band.
Favorite
Activity: Playing
my guitar.

Dan Marino
Dream: To
play football
in the NFL.
Favorite
Activity: Sports.

Grace Gunn
Dream: To own
a 1957 Chevy.
Favorite
Activity:
Repairing
my car.

Clara Klutz
Dream: To dance
in the New York
City Ballet.
Favorite
Activity:
Ballet dancing.

Alberta Einstein
Dream: To win
the Nobel Prize
for science.
Favorite
Activity: Physics
Experiments.

Ross Perot
Dream: To make
a million dollars.
Favorite
Activity:
Helping at my
dad's business.

Con Structor:
Dream: To build
my own house.
Favorite
Activity:
Carpentry.

Brian Tumor
Dream: To find a
cure for cancer.
Favorite
Activity:
Volunteering at
the hospital.

Cull T. Vator
Dream: To own
my own land in
the country.
Favorite
Activity:
Growing plants.

Alice: *Alice will perform in front of many people.*

1. Alberta:_____

2. Dan: _____

3. Grace: _____

4. Clara: _____

5. Ross: _____

6. Con: _____

7. Brian: _____

8. Cull: _____

Exercise 4 (Focus 2)

Write the questions for each of the answers using the underlined words as cues.

EXAMPLE: *Will Ross own oil wells?*

Yes, Ross'll own oil wells.

1. _____

   Alberta will win the Nobel Price for science <u>in 2021</u>.

2. _____

   Grace'll open her garage <u>in town</u>.

3. _____

   <u>No</u>, Clara will not become rich and famous.

4. _____

   Cull'll buy a tractor <u>because it will help him on the farm</u>.

5. _____

   Brian will go to medical school <u>in Boston</u>.

6. _____

   It'll take Con <u>one year</u> to build his new house.

7. _____

   Dan will play football <u>in Miami</u>.

8. _____

   <u>The Beatles</u> will discover Alice.

Exercise 5 *(Focus 3)*

Complete the dialogue with the correct form of **be going to**. The first one has been done for you as an example.

Helen: _Are you going to_ get ready for the party?

Paul: I don't want to. It_____ be fun at all. This _____ be a boring party.

Helen: It _____ be boring. It's going to be fun.

Paul: Your uncle _____ want to show his vacation slides. The slides _____ put me asleep. Then we _____ listen to him talk about everything in detail. What _____ eat for dinner?

Helen: We _____ have roast beef.

Paul: It _____ be undercooked. I _____ to eat the meat if it is too rare. Your aunt _____ eat it and then she _____ to feel well. I know she _____ get sick.

Exercise 6 *(Focus 3)*

PAIR

Ask your partner to predict the following things. Be sure to use the correct form of **be going to** in your question and answers.

E X A M P L E : Predict the weather tomorrow.

What is the weather going to be like tomorrow?

It's going to rain.

1. Predict what grade you are going to get in this class.
2. Predict when the sun is going to set tonight.
3. Predict who is going to be the next person to walk into your classroom.

Exercise 7 (Focus 4)

This is Suzy's appointment calendar. Today is September first. Use a **future time expressi**
to tell when Suzy will do the following activities.

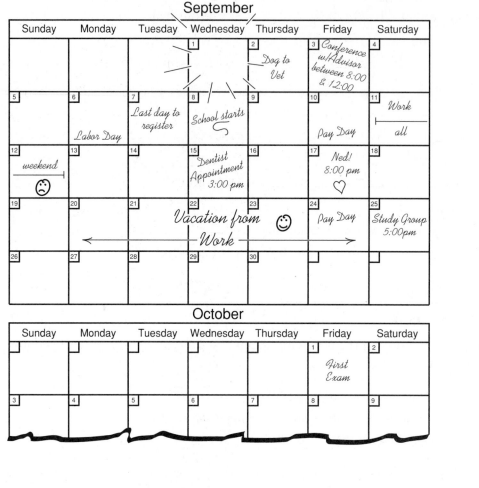

September

Sunday	Monday	Tuesday	Wednesday	Thursday	Friday	Saturday
			1	2 Dog to Vet	3 Conference w/Advisor between 8:00 & 12:00	4
5	6 Labor Day	7 Last day to register	8 School starts	9	10 Pay Day	11 Work all
12 weekend	13	14	15 Dentist Appointment 3:00 pm	16	17 Ned! 8:00 pm	18
19	20	21	22 Vacation from Work	23	24 Pay Day	25 Study Group 5:00pm
26	27	28	29	30		

October

Sunday	Monday	Tuesday	Wednesday	Thursday	Friday	Saturday
					1 First Exam	2
3	4	5	6	7	8	9

EXAMPLE: Start school
Suzy will start school

1. Meet with her study group

   _____

2. Have a dentist appointment

   _____

3. Get paid

   _____

4. Have a vacation from work

   _____

5. Have a conference with her advisor

_____

6. Have a date with Ned

_____

7. Take her first exam

_____

8. Take her dog to the vet

_____

9. Have to work all weekend

_____

Exercise 8 *(Focus 5)*

Look at Suzy's calendar again. Answer the following questions, using the correct **prepositions of time**.

1. What time does the study group meet?

_____

2. How long is Suzy's vacation from work?

_____

3. What month will she start school?

_____

4. What night will she have a date with Ned?

_____

5. What time is her dentist appointment?

_____

6. At what time should she see her advisor?

_____

7. How long is it until school begins?

_____

8. How long is it until she has to work all weekend?

_____

9. What day will she take her dog to the vet?

_____

10. Until what day can she register for classes?

_____

Exercise 9 *(Focus 6)*

Complete the dialogue with the correct form of **will** or **be going to**.

Aunt Polly: Tom Sawyer, you (1) _____ paint the fence; that is already decided.

Tom: But, Aunt Polly, I don't want to paint the fence.

Aunt Polly: I (2) _____ stand for this Tom. You (3) _____ cause my death yet. You (4) _____ do some work.

Tom: But, all the other boys (5) _____ go swimming.

Aunt Polly: Well, you (6) _____ do some painting.

Ben: Why are you carrying that bucket and brush, Tom? What (7) _____ to do?

Tom: I (8) _____ paint the fence.

Ben: Why (9) _____ to do that? I (10) _____ go swimming. You (11) _____ have any fun.

Tom: Because I like to. I (12) _____ to have fun.

Ben: Hey, that looks like fun, let me try doing it.

Tom: No, Aunt Polly (13) _____ like that. Besides I'm having fun.

Ben: Please, Tom, let me do it?

Tom: Ok, but what (14) _____ give me?

Ben: How about this apple?

Tom: Ok.

Exercise 10 *(Focus 6)*

Read the dialogue again. Write *P* above the answers which predict future events. Write *I* above the answers which **express intentions or prior plans.**

Quantifiers

Exercise 1 *(Focus 1)*

Look at the picture of the five food groups. Decide which foods pictured are **count** and which are **non-count nouns**. Write the name of each food in the proper category.

Count	Non-count

Exercise 2 (Focus 2)

Look at what Wendy Weightlifter and Skinny Sarah had for breakfast and lunch, then compl
the sentences below using *many, a lot of, some, a few, a little, few, any, no, much, very little,*
any. There is more than one correct answer for some of the blanks. Compare your answ
with a classmate. The first one has been done for you as an example.

Wendy Weightlifter		**Skinny Sarah**	
Breakfast	**Lunch**	**Breakfast**	**Lunch**
4 eggs	Chicken	Yogurt	vegetable soup
orange juice	onion rings	cup of coffee	milk
bacon	4 apples	bagel	salad
3 pieces of toast	3 sodas		grapes

Wendy had *some* eggs for breakfast. She also drank (1) _____ orange juice. She a
(2) _____ bacon. Finally, she ate (3) _____ toast.

Sarah didn't eat (4) _____ for breakfast. She had (5) _____ yogurt. She
drank (6) _____ coffee and ate a bagel with (7) _____ jam.

Wendy also had a big lunch. She ate (8) _____ of chicken, (9) _____ onio
rings and (10) _____ apples. She also drank (11) _____ soda.

Sarah didn't have (12) _____ chicken for lunch. She had (13) _____ sou
(14) _____ salad and (15) _____ grape. She drank (16) _____ milk.

Exercise 3 (Focus 2)

Write three sentences about what you ate yesterday using the quantifiers from Exercise 2.

_____

_____

_____

Exercise 4 (Focus 3)

Read the answers below, and then write the questions about what Wendy and Sarah ate. The first one has been done for you as an example.

EXAMPLE: *How many onion rings did she eat?*
She ate some onion rings.

1. _____

She drank one cup of coffee for breakfast.

2. _____

She didn't have any hot dogs for lunch.

3. _____

Wendy drank a lot of orange juice for breakfast.

4. _____

She didn't eat much food for breakfast.

5. _____

She had some vegetable soup.

6. _____

She ate four apples for lunch.

7. _____

She didn't eat any grapes for lunch.

8. _____

She didn't have any soup for lunch.

9. _____

She ate some yogurt for breakfast.

10. _____

She had a little milk for lunch.

Exercise 5 *(Focus 4)*

Wendy is training for a body-building competition. She needs to lose some weight befor
competition. She decided the best way to lose the weight would be to go to training ca
However, Wendy is not very happy at camp. Finish the letter she wrote to her mom w
few, a little, few or *little*. The first one has been done for you as an example.

Dear Mom,

I hope eveything is ok at home. I'm having *a few* problems here at training camp. I'r

glad that I only have _____ more time here. I'm ready to go home.

First, I wish we could have _____ more food. There is so _____ food at

breakfast that I'm starving by 10:00. All I had for breakfast were _____ grapes an

_____ milk and a piece of toast with _____ margarine.

Another problem is the exercise program. We are always doing something: lifting

weights, walking, swimming, riding bikes—we have _____ time to relax. At the

end of the day I have _____ energy. I can barely make it into bed. Then we have

_____ hours to sleep. They wake us up at 6:00 A.M. and we go to bed at 10:00. I

exhausted.

The only good thing is that I've made _____ friends. There are three girls in n

cabin that are also trying to lose _____ weight for the competition.

I will be home in three days. Thank goodness I only have _____ more time he

Maybe I can lose _____ weight in _____ more days on this diet.

Your daughter,

Wendy

Exercise 6 *(Focus 5)*

Wendy is home from training camp and wants to go grocery shopping. Her mother told
to make a shopping list. Look at the things Wendy is thinking of buying and write Wen
list with the correct measure word. The first one has been done for you.

a loaf of bread _____

_____

_____

_____

_____

_____

_____

138

Choose the <u>one</u> word or phrase that best completes the sentence.

1. My dog can do many tricks, but there are some things it can't do by _____.
   - (A) itself
   - (B) theirself
   - (C) herself
   - (D) myself

2. Are you thirsty? There's some lemonade in the refrigerator—Help _____.
   - (A) myself
   - (B) himself
   - (C) thierselves
   - (D) yourself

3. She fell off the skateboard and hurt _____.
   - (A) by herself
   - (B) by sheself
   - (C) herself
   - (D) sheself

4. Neither boy said who broke the window. Each blamed _____.
   - (A) themselves
   - (B) himself
   - (C) each other
   - (D) themself

5. The dance was great. We enjoyed _____.
   - (A) usselves
   - (B) ourselves
   - (C) ourself
   - (D) weself

6. I don't think you can finish that book by yourself. _____ need some help.
   - (A) Will you
   - (B) You're going to
   - (C) You going
   - (D) You are going

7. _____ win the prize for best actor?
   - (A) Who will
   - (B) Will
   - (C) When will
   - (D) Why you will

8. The almanac predicts that _____ a hurricane in August.
   - (A) there is
   - (B) it will
   - (C) there will be
   - (D) there was

9. What a beautiful morning! I feel great! This _____ a great day!
   - (A) is going to be
   - (B) will be
   - (C) is going being
   - (D) won't be

10. I _____ clean up after you. You must clean your own mess.
    - (A) am going to
    - (B) amn't going to
    - (C) 'm not going to
    - (D) isn't going to

11. _____ study in the library today? No, _____.
    - (A) Are you going to... we're not
    - (B) Are you going... I'm not
    - (C) Do you will... we won't
    - (D) Are you going to... I am

12. How_____ to get to Ohio next week?
    (A) he go   (B) are he going
    (C) does he go   (D) is he going

13. _____, we are going to see my sister's graduation ceremony.
    (A) Nowadays   (B) Usually
    (C) A week from today   (D) Last week

14. Will you please buy_____ bananas at the store?
    (A) a   (B) a little
    (C) some   (D) any

Identify the one underlined word or phrase that must be changed in order for the sentence to be grammatically correct.

15. Will have you time to go shopping for some groceries tomorrow?
          A   **B**   **C**   **D**

16. Yes, I'm going to buy some groceries. What do we need? We'm going to run out of
          A   **B**
    eggs and milk and we don't have any butter.
                      C   **D**

17. I'll pick up a very little groceries. How many eggs do we need? A dozen eggs will be
    A   **B**   **C**   **D**
    enough.

18. How many milk do we need? How much butter should I buy?
    A   **B**   **C**   **D**

19. We'll need a gallon of milk and a loaf of butter.
    A   **B**   **C**   **D**

20. Will you be able to do the shopping alone, by myself? Yes, I'll be fine. It's no trouble.
    A   **B**   **C**   **D**

21. I need some paper, but I can't reach it by myself; it's up too high. How many paper do
        A   **B**   **C**   **D**
    you need?

22. I'll get it for you. How many sheets of paper do you want? I don't need much sheets.
    A   **B**   **C**   **D**

23. What are you going do? Are you going to write something?
    A   **B**   **C**   **D**

24. No, I'm no going to write; I'm going to draw some pictures.
         A   **B**   **C**   **D**

25. What kind of pictures do you draw? I draw pictures of fruit. Will you draws a picture
                                            A   **B**   **C**
    for me? Sure—I'll get some pencils.
                      D

26. Hey, this is a nice picture of a apple, an orange, and a bunch of bananas. Did you draw
                             A   **B**   **C**
    it yourself?
     D

27. You should keep on practicing. Soon you will be a great artist. I hope so. I'll be going
                             A   **B**   **C**
    to art school on September.
          D

UNIT 25

Adjective Phrases

Exercise 1 *(Focus 1)*

Match the following sentences with the pictures they describe. Write the letter of the picture in the blank next to the sentence that describes it.

1. __ The men in the ambulance are paramedics.
2. __ The boy on the skateboard is going to crash.
3. __ The man at the stoplight is in a hurry.
4. __ The minivan on the highway is full of children.
5. __ The car with the red light on top is a police car.
6. __ The tricycle with the squeaky wheel belongs to the little girl.
7. __ The truck parked at the grocery store is full of bread.
8. __ The fire engine with the ladder is blocking the intersection.
9. __ The bulldozer with the woman driver is new.
10. __ The car with a dent is a sports car.
11. __ The elegant lady with the chauffeur owns a limousine.

a

b

c

141

d

e

f

g

h

i

j

k

Exercise 2 *(Focus 1)*

Circle the **adjective phrases** in each of the sentences in Exercise 1.

Exercise 3 *(Focus 2)*

Look at the following pictures. Each vehicle belongs to one of the people. Match each person to the appropriate vehicle. Then write sentences using **adjective phrases.**

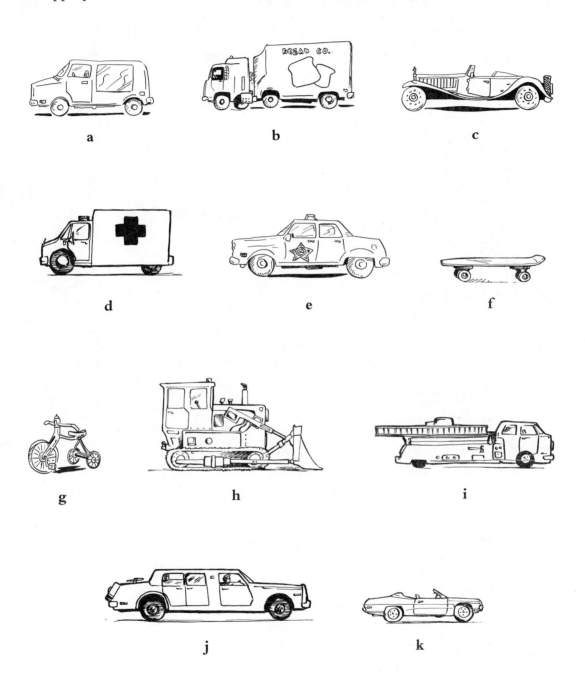

a

b

c

d

e

f

g

h

i

j

k

1. _____
2. _____
3. _____
4. _____
5. _____
6. _____
7. _____
8. _____
9. _____
10. _____
11. _____

Exercise 4 (Focus 3)

Cheryl and her daughter Rachel are going shopping for school clothes. They each have different ideas about what kind of clothes to buy. Complete the following by writing **which** questions for each answer.

1. _____

   Cheryl wants to get the long skirt.

2. _____

   Rachel likes the high heel shoes.

3. _____

   Rachel prefers long, dangling earrings.

4. _____

   Cheryl wants to buy the pullover sweater.

5. _____

   Rachel likes the skirt with holes.

6. _____

   Cheryl prefers the small earrings.

7. _____

   Rachel likes the tight blouse.

8. _____

   Rachel wants to buy the hooded sweater.

9. _____

   Cheryl wants to buy the flat shoes.

Exercise 5 *(Focus 3)*

These are the new school clothes Cheryl bought for Rachel. Take turns asking your partner which clothes they bought.

EXAMPLE: *Which earrings did they buy?*

They bought the small ones.

Phrasal Verbs

Exercise 1 *(Focus 1)*

Read the following story. Circle the phrasal verbs. The first one has been done for you as an example.

My name is Jacques Désire. I am from Haiti. I want to be a journalist, but before I can study my major I have to improve my English.

Today I went my first college class. I was a little nervous on my way to class. I drove a little too fast. I almost (ran into) another car. I told myself to calm down and slow down. Finally, I made it to class safely.

When I found the right classroom, I saw several students sitting in small groups. "Come in," said one Hispanic woman.

After I sat down the teacher came in. Immediately, I stood up, but I couldn't figure it out. None of the other students stood up. In Haiti, we always stand up when the teacher comes into the room. "Please sit down," said the teacher in a kind voice.

Then the teacher handed out some information cards. "Please fill out the card," she said, "and don't forget to include your phone number so I can call you up if I need to."

After we filled it out, the teacher handed out an information sheet about the course. The teacher went over the requirements of the class and told us to put the information sheet away in a safe place.

Exercise 2 *(Focus 2)*

Write captions for the pictures about Jacques Désire's day. Use the following verbs to help you. The first one has been done for you.

hand out   come in
stand up   run into
fill out   go over
calm down

Jacques almost runs into another car.

_____

_____

_____

_____

Exercise 3 *(Focus 3)*

Take turns with your partner. One of you read each command and the other act it out.

1. Clean up the papers on the floor, take out the trash, throw away the trash.
2. Stand up, turn on the TV, turn off the light, sit down.
3. Come in the door, take off your coat, hang up your coat, put on your sweater.
4. Come into the class, run into the desk, fall down, calm down, get up.

Comparison with Adjectives

Exercise 1 *(Focus 1)*

Use the following **adjectives** to **compare** the shoes of Bob the basketball player and Felicia the fashion model.

comfortable   old
new   expensive
big   casual
dressy

E X A M P L E :   Bob's shoes are more comfortable than Felicia's shoes.

1. _____

2. _____

3. _____

4. _____

5. _____

6. _____

Bob likes comedy movies and Felicia likes romances. Use the following adjectives to compare the movies.

emotional   exciting   sensitive
sad   funny   silly

7. _____

_____

8. _____

_____

9. _____

_____

10. _____

_____

11. _____

_____

12. _____

_____

Exercise 2 (*Focus 2*)

This is my hometown, Skagway, Alaska. It is a small, isolated town—only 700 people live there, but the people are very friendly because they all know each other. The closest town to Skagway is 50 miles away.

Skagway is a historic town. In 1898, Skagway was a gold rush town. At that time 20,000 people lived there. Most of the buildings from that time are still standing.

Every summer thousands of tourists visit Skagway to see a gold rush town and to see the spectacular beauty of the surrounding mountains.

In the winter Skagway doesn't have many tourists. It is very cold, wet, snowy, and windy, but in the summer the weather is pleasant. Because Skagway is near the Arctic Circle, the summer days are long. Sometimes the sun never sets at all.

Using the cues, write sentences comparing your hometown to Skagway.

EXAMPLE: Good winter weather

The winter weather in Miami is better than Skagway.

1. old _____

_____

2. far _____

_____

3. large _____

_____

4. historic _____

_____

5. touristic _____

_____

6. beautiful _____

_____

7. cold _____

_____

8. wet _____

_____

9. snowy _____

_____

10. windy _____

_____

11. long days _____

_____

12. bad winter weather

Exercise 3 *(Focus 2)*

GROUP

Bring pictures of your hometown or city to class. Compare the place you are from with your classmates. Tell what is better or worse about the place you are from.

Exercise 4 (Focus 3)

Interview your partner. Ask **yes/no** questions or **who**, **which**, and **whose** questions. Compare the place your partner is from with the place he or she lives in now. Use the cues to help you.

EXAMPLE: expensive

Which place is more expensive to live in, Guatemala City or New York?
New York is more expensive.

or

Is Guatemala City more expensive to live in than New York?
Yes, it is.

1. expensive
2. crowded
3. small
4. bad traffic
5. clean

6. warm
7. beautiful
8. friendly
9. bad crime
10. interesting

Exercise 5 (Focus 4)

Sheri is from Iran, but she has lived in the United States for 2 years. Sheri took the Personal Values Inventory which compares US values with values of some other countries.

A. Look at Sheri's responses to the Personal Values Inventory and write sentences expressing **similarities** and **differences**. The first one has been done for you.

Personal Values Inventory

US Values		Some Other Countries' Values
Innovative	X———————|————————	Traditional
Action Oriented	├———————|————————X	"Being" Oriented
Individualistic	├———————|————————X	Group Oriented
Competitive	├———————|————————X	Cooperative
Future Oriented	X———————|————————	Past Oriented
Informal	├———————|————————X	Formal
Direct	X———————|————————	Indirect

E X A M P L E :   Sheri is as innovative as people from the United States. She isn't as traditional
as people from some other countries.

1. _____
   _____

2. _____
   _____

3. _____
   _____

4. _____
   _____

5. _____
   _____

6. _____
   _____

B. Do the Personal Values Inventory for yourself. Then write sentences expressing similarities
and differences for your own values.

Personal Values Inventory

US Values		Some Other Countries' Values
Innovative	├──────────┼──────────┤	Traditional
Action Oriented	├──────────┼──────────┤	"Being" Oriented
Individualistic	├──────────┼──────────┤	Group Oriented
Competitive	├──────────┼──────────┤	Cooperative
Future Oriented	├──────────┼──────────┤	Past Oriented
Informal	├──────────┼──────────┤	Formal
Direct	├──────────┼──────────┤	Indirect

E X A M P L E :   I am just as innovative as people from the United States.

1. _____
   _____

2. _____
   _____

3. _____
   _____

4. _____
   _____

5. _____

_____

6. _____

_____

7. _____

_____

Exercise 6 (Focus 5)

Mitchell and Manny are competing in the Mr. All-American contest. Betty Blunt and Polly Polite are the judges of the contest. Look at the score sheet below. Write sentences comparing the two contestants using both the **direct** and **polite** forms. The first one has been done for you.

	Manners	Talent	Singing	Intelligence	Sports
Mitchell	9	9	8	10	3
Manny	5	7	3	8	10

E X A M P L E : (good/singing) Betty: *Manny sings worse than Mitchell.*

Polly: *Manny is not as good at singing as Mitchell.*

1. (tall) Betty: _____

Polly: _____

2. (muscular) Betty: _____

Polly: _____

3. (talented) Betty: _____

Polly: _____

4. (thin) Betty: _____

Polly: _____

5. (intelligent) Betty: _____

Polly: _____

6. (athletic) Betty: _____

Polly: _____

7. (good/dressed) Betty: _____

Polly: _____

TOEFL® Test Preparation
Exercises · Units 25–27

Choose the <u>one</u> word or phrase that best completes the sentence.

1. I am going to _____ my grandfather at the train station. Do you want to come?
    (A) hand out
    (B) put down
    (C) pick up
    (D) fill out

2. Sure, but first you should _____ the station and _____ if the train is on time.
    (A) call up . . . find out
    (B) open up . . . see
    (C) call in . . . hand out
    (D) turn on . . . turn off

3. The train is on time. _____ car should we take—the compact _____ ? Let's take the van.
    (A) What . . . and the Van
    (B) Which . . . or the van
    (C) What . . . the van
    (D) Which . . . with the van

4. My grandfather is 95, but he looks like he's 60. He's _____ he looks.
    (A) as old as
    (B) younger than
    (C) older than
    (D) as young as

5. _____ is your grandfather?
    (A) What person
    (B) What one
    (C) Which person
    (D) When

6. The man with all the suitcases _____ my grandfather.
    (A) are
    (B) were
    (C) to be
    (D) is

7. The suitcases he is holding _____ some surprises.
    (A) contain
    (B) contains
    (C) contained
    (D) has

8. I'm not sure what is in those suitcases, but he doesn't _____ anything.
    (A) throw up
    (B) throw away
    (C) throw over
    (D) throw in

9. It's lucky you drove the van, it's a _____ car than your compact.
    (A) biger
    (B) more big
    (C) biggest
    (D) bigger

10. It's _____ the small car, but it is better for carrying a lot of stuff and I know Grandpa always has a lot of stuff.
    (A) noisy than
    (B) more noisily than
    (C) noisiest than
    (D) noisier than

11. Will I like your grandfather? Sure, you'll like him. He's the _____ man I know.
   (A) more interesting   (B) most interesting
   (C) interestingest   (D) more interesting than

12. What do you have in all those suitcases, Grandpa? I hope it's not clothes. It will take u[
   a long time to _____ .
   (A) hang up them   (B) hang them up
   (C) put them up   (D) put up them

13. Don't worry, granddaughter, it's not that much. Most of the suitcases are _____
   they look.
   (A) as light as   (B) lighter
   (C) lighter than   (D) lighter then

14. You're right. They are _____ I expected. What's in them?
   (A) not as heavy as   (B) heavier than
   (C) not as light   (D) as difficult

15. Some fresh air from the countryside. Country air is _____ city air.
   (A) refreshinger than   (B) more refreshing
   (C) most refreshing   (D) more refreshing than

Identify the one underlined word or phrase that must be changed in order for the sentenc[
to be grammatically correct.

16. The woman in the plaid shirt is leaving her campsite. She is putting her campfire on.
                A   B   C   D

17. Where are the information forms with the students' names on them? I handed out then[
          A   B   C   D
   already.

18. Calm down, don't worry about the test. It is more easy than the last one.
       A   B   C   D

19. The lady with the radio is very noisy. We are trying to make her quieter. We are alway[
           A   B   C
   telling her to turn up the music.
             D

20. Please, turn on the lights. Thanks, that is good than before. It was getting dark.
          A   B C   D

21. The United States is not as bigger as Canada in area. But the United States i[
                  A   B   C
   more populated than Canada.
       D

22. The United States has a larger population than Canada. Canada has fewer large citie[
                  A   B   C
   than the United States.
    D

23. The government of Canada is as democratic than the government of the United States
                          A B   C   D

156

24. The government with a prime minister is Canada. However, Canada is not lest democratic
    $\underline{\qquad}$ **A**   **B** **C**   **D**
    than the United States.

25. In both countries, every worker pays taxes and fill out a tax form every year.
         A   **B**   **C**   **D**

26. Health care service is more available in Canada than the United States. Canada's health
         A   **B**
    care system is best than the U.S. system.
         C **D**

27. Usually the temperature is more cooler in Canada than in most parts of the United States.
    A   **B**   **C**   **D**

28. Canada is one of the coldest contries in the world. It is farrer north than the United
         A   **B**   **C**   **D**
    States.

29. Canada has less official languages than the United States. Canada has two official lan-
         A   **B**   **C**
    guages: English and French. The United States has no official language.
         D

30. Canadians and Americans get on well. Americans are just as friendly as Canadians.
         A   **B** **C** **D**

Comparison with Adverbs

Exercise 1 (Focus 1)

What are the differences between boys and girls? Read the questions below. Check the box that shows your opinion.

	Boys	Girls
1. Who plays jokes more often?		
2. Who works harder?		
3. Who studies more seriously?		
4. Who listens more carefully?		
5. Who gets hurt more often?		
6. Who acts more calmly?		
7. Who cries frequently?		
8. Who sings more beautifully?		
9. Who observes more closely?		
10. Who draws more artistically?		

Exercise 2 (Focus 1)

Using your opinions from Exercise 1, write a sentence using the **comparative forms of the adverbs.**

E X A M P L E : *Girls play jokes more often than boys.*

1. _____

2. _____

3. _____

4. _____

5. _____

6. _____

7. _____

8. _____

9. _____

10. _____

Exercise 3 *(Focus 2)*

A. Pia and Dan are twins. Using the cues, write sentences which tell how they are **similar** or **different.**

E X A M P L E : (draw/creative) *Pia draws more creatively than Dan.*

1. (spell/good) _____
2. (read/quick) _____
3. (write/neat) _____
4. (talk/quiet) _____
5. (answer/polite) _____

B. Nathan and Ned are athletes. They are also alike in many ways. Using the cues, write sentences which tell how they are **similar** or **different**.

| Nathan | | | | | | |
Sunday	Monday	Tuesday	Wednesday	Thursday	Friday	Saturday
31 practice	1 practice	2 practice	3 practice	4 practice	5 practice	6 practice
7 practice	8 practice	9 practice	10 practice	11 practice	12 practice	13 practice

| Ned | | | | | | |
Sunday	Monday	Tuesday	Wednesday	Thursday	Friday	Saturday
31	1 practice	2	3 practice	4	5 practice	6
7	8 practice	9	10 practice	11	12 practice	13

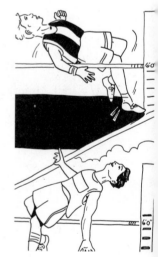

6. (jump/high) _____

7. (run/fast) _____

8. (throw/far) _____

9. (practice/frequent) _____

10. (practice/hard) _____

Exercise 4 (Focus 3)

Steve is the owner of Water Trails Kayak Club. Cynthia and her daughter Mariah want to join the kayak club, but first Cynthia has to answer a few questions. Look at the information card Steve has to fill out. Write the questions he asks. The first one has been done for you as an example.

Club Member

Name <u>Cynthia Schuemann</u>

Age _____

Swimming ability _____

Kayaking ability _____

Number of years kayaking _____

How often kayaking planned _____

Distance to kayak _____

Distance to kayak
club from home _____

Length of Membership:

_____ 6 months _____ 1 year

Method of payment:

_____ check _____ cash

_____ credit card

1. How *old are you?*

2. How _____

3. How _____

4. How _____

5. How _____

6. How _____

7. How _____

8. How _____

9. How _____

Related Family Member

Name <u>Mariah Schuemann</u>

Age _____

Swimming ability _____

Kayaking ability _____

Number of years kayaking _____

How often kayaking planned _____

Distance to kayak _____

10. How old _____

11. How _____

12. How _____

13. How _____

14. How _____

15. How _____

UNIT 29

Superlatives

Exercise 1 *(Focus 1)*

How much do you know about the country of Canada? Match the information in the two columns below. The first one has been done for you as an example.

_C_ the longest river		A. Quebec
— the tallest mountain		B. the Prime Minister
— the longest waterfall		C. the Milk River
— the largest lake		D. the CN tower
— the biggest city		E. Mount Logan
— the tallest building		F. Toronto
— the oldest city		G. the United States
— the highest government official		H. Alert, the Northwest Territories
— the town that is the farthest north		I. Lake Superior
— the earliest European explorer		J. Della Falls
— the biggest trading partner		K. Jacques Cartier

Exercise 2 *(Focus 1)*

Using the information from Exercise 1, write five sentences about Canada.

EXAMPLE: *The Milk River is the longest river in Canada.*

1. _____
2. _____
3. _____
4. _____
5. _____

162

Exercise 3 (Focus 1 and 2)

Think of all the people you know. Write the name of a person who is at the top of the group next to each category. Write a sentence with the correct form of the superlative. Be careful to spell the superlative correctly.

EXAMPLES: tall *Jim*
           Jim is the tallest.
           or
           writes neatly *Diane*
           Diane writes the most neatly.

1. silly _____

    _____

2. sleepy _____

    _____

3. runs quickly _____

    _____

4. helpful _____

    _____

5. sleeps lightly _____

    _____

6. pleasant _____

    _____

7. heavy _____

    _____

8. busy _____

    _____

9. sad _____

    _____

10. drives slowly _____

    _____

11. good musician _____

    _____

12. graceful dancer _____

    _____

13. has blue eyes _____

_____

14. works hard _____

_____

Exercise 4 *(Focus 1 and 2)*

Do the same as in Exercise 3, except this time write the name of a person who is at th
bottom of the group next to each category.

1. bad writer _____

_____

2. shy _____

_____

3. interesting _____

_____

4. busy _____

_____

5. sings badly _____

_____

Exercise 5 *(Focus 3)*   PAI

Find out about your partner's native country. Use the cues to ask him or her questions, usin
one of the. Record your partner's answers. Answer the questions in complete sentences.

E X A M P L E : famous landmarks

What is one of the most famous landmarks in your country?

The Statue of Liberty is one of the most famous landmarks in my country.

1. famous landmarks

_____

2. best restaurants

_____

3. most interesting sights

_____

4. least expensive places to shop

_____

5. longest rivers

_____

6. most common foods

_____

7. biggest industries

_____

8. warmest places to visit

_____

9. greatest artists or entertainers

_____

10. best times to visit

_____

11. most beautiful cities

_____

Exercise 6 *(Focus 3)* GROUP

Tell what you learned from Exercise 5 about your partner's country to the rest of your classmates. If there are students from the same country as your partner, ask them if they agree with your partner's answers.

E X A M P L E : *I learned that one of the longest rivers in Brazil is the Amazon River.*

Factual Conditional

Exercise 1 *(Focus 1)*

Read the statements below. If the statement is true, circle "T". If the statement is false, circle "F" and rewrite the statement below so it is true. The first one has been done for you as an example.

T (F) **1.** If you mix yellow and red, you get green.

T F **2.** If you are on the equator, the sun rises and sets at the same time every day.

T F **3.** If you don't get enough sleep, you never get sick.

T F **4.** If a tadpole grows up, it becomes a butterfly.

T F **5.** If you scuba dive under water, you need an oxygen tank.

T F **6.** If there are 366 days in a year, it is a leap year.

T F **7.** If you eat too many fatty foods, you lose weight.

T F **8.** If your skin is exposed to too much sun, you get a sunburn.

T F **9.** If plants don't have sunlight, they grow faster.

T F **10.** If it is winter, ducks migrate.

T F **11.** If a surface is smooth, it has less friction than a rough surface.

Correct sentences

1. *If you mix yellow and red, you get orange.*

2. _____

3. _____

4. _____

5. _____

6. _____

7. _____

8. _____

9. _____

10. _____

11. _____

Exercise 2 *(Focus 2)*

Tell what you do **habitually** in the following situations.

EXAMPLE: When you want to be alone
If I want to be alone, I go to my bedroom.

1. When you want to be alone

   _____

2. When you need a quiet place to study

   _____

3. Who takes care of you when you are sick

   _____

4. When you want to be with people

   _____

5. When you are caught in a heavy rain

   _____

6. When you have too much stress in your life

   _____

7. When you don't have enough money to buy what you want

   _____

8. When you don't feel like cooking dinner

   _____

9. When you have a bad day

   _____

10. When you get a good grade on a test

    _____

Exercise 3 (Focus 3)

A. Remember what happened when you were a teenager. How did your parents treat you i
each of the following situations? Complete the following statements.

EXAMPLE: If you came home late

If I came home late, my parents didn't let me go out again.

1. If you came home late

   _____

2. If you got good grades in school

   _____

3. If you wanted new clothes

   _____

4. If you didn't clean your room

   _____

5. If you needed some money

   _____

6. If you wanted to go on a date

   _____

B. Are you different from your parents? How do you treat your children? (If you don't hav
children, imagine that you do.)

EXAMPLE: If your son/daughter comes home late

If my daughter comes home late, I ground her.

7. If your son/daughter comes home late

   _____

8. If your son/daughter gets good grades in school

   _____

9. If your son/daughter wants new clothes

   _____

10. If your son/daughter doesn't clean his/her room

    _____

11. If your son/daughter needs some money

    _____

12. If your son/daughter wants to go on a date

    _____

Exercise 4 *(Focus 3)*

Compare your answers for questions 1–6 with 7–12 in Exercise 3. Explain to your partner why your answers are the same or different.

Exercise 5 *(Focus 4)*

Answer the questions below using an *if* clause or *when(ever)* in the second position.

EXAMPLE: When does water freeze?
            Water freezes whenever it is 0° C.

1.   How do you get good grades in school?

     _____

2.   When were you motivated in school?

     _____

3.   When do you get frustrated?

     _____

4.   How do seeds grow into plants?

     _____

5.   When does it snow?

     _____

6.   When do you cook a big dinner?

     _____

7.   When do you go on vacation?

     _____

8.   When do you feel homesick?

     _____

9.   How do you make the color orange?

     _____

Choose the one word or phrase that best completes the sentence.

1. _____ take you to drive to work?
   - (A) How does it
   - (B) How long is it
   - (C) How long does it
   - (D) How far does it

2. It depends. If I _____ my house early, it only _____ 30 minutes.
   - (A) leave...takes
   - (B) left...takes
   - (C) am leaving...is taking
   - (D) leave...took

3. If I leave my house by 6:00 A.M. I can get to work before my boss _____ .
   - (A) is
   - (B) will
   - (C) can
   - (D) does

4. At 6:00 A.M. I can drive _____ than at 6:30 because there is less traffic.
   - (A) quick
   - (B) quicker
   - (C) more quickly
   - (D) most quickly

5. The early drivers are nice; they _____ the later drivers.
   - (A) don't drive as crazily as
   - (B) drive as crazy as
   - (C) don't drive crazy
   - (D) aren't driving crazy

6. They also drive _____ than the later drivers do.
   - (A) carefulest
   - (B) carefully
   - (C) most carefully
   - (D) more carefully

7. Also, the early drivers don't yell, and they honk their horns _____ .
   - (A) most frequently
   - (B) less frequently
   - (C) frequenter
   - (D) not frequently

8. One of _____ things of all about late drivers is that they don't pay attention.
   - (A) worse
   - (B) the baddest
   - (C) the worst
   - (D) worse than

9. Late drivers put on their makeup or shave while they're driving _____ early drivers.
   - (A) more often
   - (B) more often than
   - (C) the most often
   - (D) more than

10. They are _____ drivers of all.
    - (A) more dangerous than
    - (B) the dangerousest
    - (C) the most dangerous
    - (D) most dangerous

11. Once I saw a man reading while he was driving. I'm sure he was the _____ driver of all.

    (A) most careful   (B) least careful

    (C) very careful   (D) less careful than

12. _____ you have to drive?

    (A) How farther do   (B) How far

    (C) How farthest do   (D) How far do

13. It's only 18 miles _____ a short cut.

    (A) whenever I took   (B) if I am taking

    (C) if I take   (D) when taking

14. I know it's the same distance no matter what time I leave, but if I leave later it seems _____ when I leave early.

    (A) farther than   (B) the furthest

    (C) farrer than   (D) far

15. No one at my job travels as far as _____ .

    (A) I can   (B) I will

    (C) I do   (D) I am

Identify the one underlined word or phrase that must be changed in order for the sentence to be correct.

16. Whenever you fly from Europe to North America you lose time.
                A   **B**   **C**   **D**

17. If it is noon in London, it was 6 A.M. in Montreal.
     A B   **C**   **D**

18. One of the difficultest things about traveling across the Atlantic Ocean is jet lag.
           A   **B**   **C**   **D**

19. The good and fastest way to get over jet lag is to plan ahead.
        A **B**   **C**   **D**

20. If the time change is more than six hours, your sense of time was distorted.
    A   **B**   **C**   **D**

21. You will do everything very sleepily during the day, and act more alert at night.
                    A   **B**   **C**   **D**

22. The goodest advice I can give you is to make the change as slowly as possible. Don't
         A   **B**   **C**

    try to stay awake if you're very sleepy.
                        D

23. We must treat our oceans' resources more thoughtfully then we have in the past.
           A   **B**   **C**   **D**

24. Governments need to work more closely with their citizens than they do now. They
                       A   **B**

    must preserve marine life more carefullier.
                      C   **D**

25. Fishermen can understand well than most people what is happening.
           A   **B** **C**   **D**

26. Large groups of fish appear least frequently than in the past.
         A   B   C   D

27. Ocean pollution ruins life just as effectively than overfishing.
                    A   B   C   D

28. Oil spills are larger today than in the past; they pollute oceans most frequently than befo
              A   B   C   D

29. Concerned citizens complain loudly than before about the problems of the oceans.
       A   B   C   D

30. They remind us that oceans are the one of our most precious resources.
                              A B   C   D